CliffsNotes™
Taking and
Sharing Digital
Photographs

By Ken Milburn

IN THIS BOOK

- Determine the correct lighting indoors and out for taking the best digital photos

- Transfer your photos to your computer and send them to your friends and family

- Post your digital photos on your Web page

- Correct problems like red eye with the click of a mouse

- Reinforce what you learn with CliffsNotes Review

- Find more Digital Photography information in CliffsNotes Resource Center and online at www.cliffsnotes.com

IDG Books Worldwide, Inc.
An International Data Group Company
Foster City, CA • Chicago, IL • Indianapolis, IN • New York, NY

About the Author

Ken Milburn is a digital imaging expert, as well as an experienced author of many books and articles on computer graphics. He has decades of experience as an advertising and editorial photographer who started working in conventional photography and now works exclusively in digital media.

Publisher's Acknowledgments

Editorial

Senior Project Editor: Seta Frantz

Acquisitions Editor: Michael Roney

Editorial Manager, Freelance: Constance Carlisle

Copy Editor: Diana Conover

Proof Editor: Teresa Artman

Technical Editor: Alfred DeBat

Production

Indexer: York Production Services, Inc.

Proofreader: York Production Services, Inc.

IDG Books Indianapolis Production Department

Distributed by CDG Books Canada Inc. for Canada; by Transworld Publishers Limited in the United Kingdom; by IDG Norge Books for Norway; by IDG Sweden Books for Sweden; by IDG Books Australia Publishing Corporation Pty. Ltd. for Australia and New Zealand; by TransQuest Publishers Pte Ltd. for Singapore, Malaysia, Thailand, Indonesia, and Hong Kong; by Gotop Information Inc. for Taiwan; by ICG Muse, Inc. for Japan; by Intersoft for South Africa; by Eyrolles for France; by International Thomson Publishing for Germany, Austria and Switzerland; by Distribuidora Cuspide for Argentina; by LR International for Brazil; by Galileo Libros for Chile; by Ediciones ZETA S.C.R. Ltda. for Peru; by WS Computer Publishing Corporation, Inc., for the Philippines; by Contemporanea de Ediciones for Venezuela; by Express Computer Distributors for the Caribbean and West Indies; by Micronesia Media Distributor, Inc. for Micronesia; by Chips Computadoras S.A. de C.V. for Mexico; by Editorial Norma de Panama S.A. for Panama; by American Bookshops for Finland.

For general information on IDG Books Worldwide's books in the U.S., please call our Consumer Customer Service department at 800-762-2974. For reseller information, including discounts and premium sales, please call our Reseller Customer Service department at 800-434-3422.

For information on where to purchase IDG Books Worldwide's books outside the U.S., please contact our International Sales department at 317-575-3993 or fax 317-572-4002.

For consumer information on foreign language translations, please contact our Customer Service department at 1-800-434-3422, fax 317-572-4002, or e-mail rights@idgbooks.com.

For information on licensing foreign or domestic rights, please phone +1-650-653-7098.

For sales inquiries and special prices for bulk quantities, please contact our Order Services department at 800-434-3422 or write to the address above.

For information on using IDG Books Worldwide's books in the classroom or for ordering examination copies, please contact our Educational Sales department at 800-434-2086 or fax 317-572-4005.

For press review copies, author interviews, or other publicity information, please contact our Public Relations department at 650-653-7000 or fax 650-653-7500. For authorization to photocopy items for corporate, personal, or educational use, please contact Copyright Clearance Center, 222 Rosewood Drive, Danvers, MA 01923, or fax 978-750-4470.

 is a registered trademark under exclusive
license to IDG Books Worldwide, Inc.
from International Data Group, Inc.

Table of Contents

INTRODUCTION

The combination of digital cameras, computers, and software that lets you enhance, perfect, and personalize photographs has revolutionized the art and practice of photography. Ironically, this has been especially true since affordable and easy-to-use digital cameras have become plentiful — and that has only happened over the course of the last couple of years.

Yet despite the fact that digital photography has become both accessible and easy to use, few people are aware of the extent to which digital photography has gained in popularity and functionality. One of the reasons for this is that digital images can be hard to distinguish in quality from ordinary photographs, so most of us haven't been aware that more and more of the photos we see are produced without film or film processing. Digital photography also means instant gratification. You can see what you photographed within seconds of taking the picture. This book brings you an overview of affordable digital photography: What you can expect from it, what you need to know, and what you might consider buying in order to enhance your experience.

Why Do You Need This Book?

Can you answer yes to any of these questions?

- Need to know about using consumer grade digital cameras and how to get prints from them fast?

- Don't have time to read 500 pages on advanced techniques for digital photography?

- Need to know the basic rules for taking good pictures?

- Want to know how to get your digital photos onto the Web?

- Need to know what to expect from the equipment you've got?

If so, then CliffsNotes *Taking and Sharing Digital Photographs* is for you!

How to Use This Book

You're the boss here. You get to decide how to use this book. You can either read the book from cover to cover or just look for the information you want and put it back on the shelf for later. However, I'll tell you about a few ways I recommend to search for your topics:

- Use the index in the back of the book to find what you're looking for.

- Flip through the book looking for your topic in the running heads.

- Look for your topic in the Table of Contents in the front of the book.

- Look at the In This Chapter list at the beginning of each chapter.

- Look for additional information in the Resource Center, or test your knowledge in the Review section.

- Or flip through the book until you find what you're looking for — because we organized the book in a logical, task-oriented way.

Also, to find important information quickly, you can look for icons strategically placed in the text. Here is a description of the icons you'll find in this book:

If you see a Remember icon, make a mental note of this text — it's worth keeping in mind.

If you see a Tip icon, you'll know that you've run across a helpful hint, uncovered a secret, or received good advice.

The Warning icon alerts you to something that could be dangerous, requires special caution, or should be avoided.

Don't Miss Our Web Site

Keep up with the *dynamically changing* world of digital photography by visiting the CliffsNotes Web site at www.cliffsnotes.com. Here's what you find:

■ Interactive tools that are fun and informative.

■ Links to interesting Web sites.

■ Additional resources to help you continue your learning.

At www.cliffsnotes.com, you can even register for a new feature called CliffsNote-A-Day, which offers you newsletters on a variety of topics, delivered right to your e-mail in-box each business day.

If you haven't yet discovered the Internet and are wondering how to get online, pick up CliffsNotes *Getting On the Internet*, new from CliffsNotes. You'll learn just what you need to make your online connection quickly and easily. See you at www.cliffsnotes.com!

CHAPTER 1
UNDERSTANDING YOUR DIGITAL CAMERA

IN THIS CHAPTER

- Finding out what your digital camera can do
- Calculating your camera's ability to "capture the moment"
- Understanding how much detail your camera can capture
- Understanding the advantage of a zoom lens
- Controlling image quality
- Using your digital film card or onboard memory
- Using special camera functions

The Benefits of a Digital Camera

I'm assuming that you've already bought your camera. You'll have a better idea of what to expect from your camera if you understand the essential benefits of digital photography:

- Film costs nothing.
- You see your pictures even quicker than when using a Polaroid camera.

No film and processing costs

Digital cameras record the image onto rerecordable memory chips that can be erased after the pictures have been transferred to a computer. You can then use the same memory chips to record more pictures. You can repeat this shoot-record-transfer-erase cycle as often as you like.

You see your picture quicker than when using a Polaroid camera

All but the very lowest-priced digital cameras enable you to "play back" pictures on the camera's display screen as soon as you've taken them. You can even erase the pictures you don't like. Your camera may also give you an option to preview the picture while you shoot.

Calculating Your Camera's Capability to "Capture the Moment"

One of the major differences between regular cameras and their digital counterparts is that regular cameras take the picture at the exact instant when the shutter button hits bottom. Digital cameras have a delay between the instant you fully depress the shutter release button and the instant the picture is recorded. This delay is called *shutter lag*. Less shutter lag means that you're more likely to capture the exact intended moment. Older and less-expensive digital cameras tend to have more shutter lag and are better suited to photographing more inanimate subjects.

If your camera has an option to make the shutter-click audible (usually a Sound On command), you can practice anticipating the moment of shutter click. Your ability to capture the exact moment intended will improve greatly.

Understanding How Much Detail Your Camera Can Capture

The degree to which your camera is able to faithfully reproduce fine detail is dependent on the number of *pixels* (picture elements — dots of a single color and brightness) contained in a single frame. This number is called the camera's *resolution*, and it is usually expressed as *megapixels* (millions of pixels). Lower-resolution cameras use the equivalent of computer screen resolution standards, such as VGA (640 pixels wide by 480 pixels high), EGA (800 x 600 pixels), or XGA (1024 x 768 pixels). A correlation exists between these numbers and the size print you can expect to produce at the quality you've come to expect from a photograph, as shown in Table 1-1.

Table 1-1:   Camera Resolution and Maximum Print Size

Resolution	Print Size
VGA (640 x 480 pixels)	3' x 2'
EGA (800 x 600 pixels)	3.5' x 2.5'
XGA (1024 x 768 pixels)	4.25' x 3.25'
One megapixel	6' x 4'
Two megapixel	8' x 10'
Three megapixel	11' x 14'

If you are shooting for Web use, having a choice of shooting at resolutions as low as 640 x 480 pixels has benefits: more images on a storage card and less time spent preparing images for Web publication.

Some cameras are advertised as producing a higher resolution image than their image capture devices are actually capable of recording. In fact, the camera has internally re-sized (interpolated) the image. When reading the camera's literature, look for "optical resolution" on the camera's specification sheet.

Getting the Framing You Expect

Most digital cameras have optical viewfinders that permit you to view and frame the subject through an optical "window" in the camera. If you choose a camera with a zoom lens, the optical viewfinder should zoom to show the proper picture area at all zoom lens settings. However, optical viewfinders are not directly in line with the camera lens, so close-ups are likely to be misframed. Also, because most optical viewfinders don't focus, judging the nearest and farthest objects in the image that are in sharp focus (*depth of field*) is impossible.

If you are taking close-up pictures within four or five feet of your subject, use the camera's preview screen (called the *LCD*, for Liquid Crystal Display) as your viewfinder. If you are shooting outdoors, you may need to throw a jacket over your head and the camera (but not the lens) so that the image on the LCD isn't washed out by the sun.

Digital cameras use batteries much faster when the LCD is turned on. Carry an extra set of batteries.

If you wear glasses, a built-in diopter adjustment on your optical viewfinder will allow you to adjust the optics to your prescription so that you can see a sharp image.

Understanding the Advantage of a Zoom Lens

Zoom lenses make it possible to frame your image in the camera, rather than having to throw away resolution by cropping it afterwards in an image-processing program. Because consumer and *prosumer* (short for professional-level consumer — the hip new way of saying "serious hobbyist") digital cameras have only a fraction of the resolution of film, excessive trimming (*cropping*) results in unacceptable print quality.

Most of the fixed-focal-length digital cameras have wide-angle lenses that make filling the frame with a portrait or product shot nearly impossible without dramatically exaggerating perspective.

Some cameras claim to have a "Digital Zoom." "Digital Zoom" provides little benefit. The term is marketing speak for saying that the camera can resize your image internally. You simply enlarge pixels in the digital-zoom resizing process, but your image-processing software can do a much better job of resizing images.

Controlling Image Quality

Exposure refers to the amount of light used to record images, which is a factor of the length of time and the intensity of light that strikes the *image sensor* (film). Exposure determines the overall lightness or darkness of a given image. Your camera may determine exposure with or without enabling you to intervene. If exposure is fully automatic, you'll have to make any adjustments in your image-editing program. If your camera offers other exposure modes (see your camera's manual), the following table will help you to understand their purpose.

Table 1-2:   When to Use an Exposure Mode

Mode	*Purpose*
Auto	Insures that you get a viewable (if less than perfect) picture with no forethought needed as to settings.
Aperture priority	When you want to throw the background out of focus. You specify the aperture; the camera sets the shutter speed.
Shutter priority	When you want to freeze or blur motion. You choose the shutter speed; the camera sets the appropriate aperture.
Over/under	You augment or subtract the amount of light reaching the sensor in whatever increments the camera allows. Digital cameras typically allow + or - 3 *f-stops* (the numbers designating the size of the aperture) in half-stop increments. Camera chooses aperture and shutter speed.
Program	Exposure is adjusted according to considerations typical for common shooting situations. For instance, snowscapes, nightshots, and sports.
Manual	You choose the specific aperture and shutter settings according to the dictates of your experience in dealing with a given situation. All pros will insist on this.

Using exposure modes and understanding ISO ratings

A camera's *ISO rating* indicates the camera (or film's) sensitivity to light according to international standards. If you're lucky, you will be able to choose from a range of possible ISO settings. Most digital cameras have an ISO rating of about 100. Some cameras let you choose one or more higher ISO ratings — usually at the cost of slightly compromised image detail.

Warning

You should use the lowest ISO rating consistent with getting an acceptable image given the situation you're working in. Higher ISO settings almost invariably mean "grainier" images.

Understanding aperture and shutter range

You will have a much easier time determining correct exposure if you understand the meaning and purpose of aperture (f-stop) and shutter speed.

Aperture controls the overall amount of light entering the lens while the shutter controls that amount of time that light is allowed to expose the film. It is the combination of aperture and shutter speed that determine the following:

■ **Exposure:** This is the overall brightness of the recorded image, as determined by the combination of aperture setting (f-stop) and shutter speed used when the image is being photographed.

■ **Depth of field:** This is the distance between the closest and most distant objects in sharp focus. The smaller the aperture, the greater the depth of field.

■ **Whether action is frozen:** The smaller the fraction of a second the shutter is open, the more likely action will be frozen.

Using metering options

How you use the light meter in your camera (all under-$1000 digital cameras have automatic built-in light meters) will determine what information your camera uses to guess at the appropriate exposure settings. The more you pay for your camera, the more metering options you're likely to have. What the various options are and what they can do for you are outlined in Table 1-3:

**Table 1-3:   Metering Options and
             When to Choose Them**

Option	Purpose
Auto	Quick and Dirty: Camera averages the brightness of all the light it sees over a wide-angle field-of-view.
Center-weighted	Better suited to typical shooting situations where the center of interest is closest to the center of the picture. Bases about 75 percent of exposure on the central 30 percent (or so) of the image in the viewfinder.
Spot	Best for portraits, still lifes, and night shots, where only small areas contain the important details (such as skin tones in the highlight areas). Measures only about 3 percent of the image from its center.
Matrix	Best for landscapes, crowd scenes, and scenes that have areas of exceptional brightness or darkness. Divides the screen into various light-sensitive areas; then uses a complex formula to determine how much each of these areas influences the final exposure.

If you want to use center-weighted or spot metering on an area that won't be in the center of the picture, follow these steps:

1. Start by placing that object in the center of the frame.

2. Depress and hold the shutter button partway to lock the exposure.

3. Then reframe the image and finish depressing the shutter button.

Understanding Your Digital Film Card or Onboard Memory

A few digital cameras (usually the very least expensive) have only their built-in memory. Most digital cameras have one of four types of removable memory cards (measured in megabytes, often abbreviated as MB), as shown in Table 1-4:

Table 1-4: Memory Card Types, Capacities, and Advantages

Type	Current Maximum Capacity	Advantages
CompactFlash	256MB	Small; rugged; high-capacity; programmable; also used in some PDAs and MP3 players.
CompactFlash II	360MB	Slightly thicker than CompactFlash; even higher capacity; backwards-compatible with CompactFlash; can hold small hard drives.
SmartMedia	128MB	Smallest and least expensive but more easily damaged.
Memory Stick	128MB	Smallest of all. Purposely designed by Sony to be used in a very wide range of personal electronics and computing devices. So far, Sony is the only maker of digital cameras that use the Memory Stick.

Ways to Download Images to Your Computer

You can download the images from your camera to your computer in two different ways: Directly through a cable, or by using a separate external card reader to read your removable memory cards. Direct downloading can be very slow if your connection is limited to serial ports. Many newer cameras have USB (Universal Serial Bus) ports, which are several times faster (4MB per second) than serial ports. If your camera has a USB connection, it will be loudly advertised by your camera's manufacturer.

USB is a relatively new peripheral interface that has been implemented on recent models of both Macintosh and Windows-based computers. It affords several advantages over the old serial, parallel, and SCSI port alternatives:

- Faster data transfer (except for advanced versions of SCSI).

- Cross-platform adaptability of most devices.

- Up to 127 devices can be connected to the same computer.

- Devices can be attached and detached without quitting a program or turning off the computer.

- Attached devices can be turned off and on at any time without affecting the performance of the computer or other USB attached devices.

External card readers download images from your camera much faster than you can download images via a cable. In order of speed of transfer, card readers can be attached to the following types of I/O (input/output) ports: parallel port (compatible only with Windows computers), USB (very fast and works with both Mac and Windows USB-equipped computers), and SCSI (speed depends on specific class of technology, but cross-platform compatible).

Using Special Camera Functions

Your camera may have some special *firmware* (built-in software) features that can be quite useful. Those that you're (so far) most likely to find are described in the following paragraphs.

Burst mode

This firmware feature enables you to take a series of pictures in rapid sequence with one press of the shutter button. Burst mode can be very handy for making frames for GIF animations (see Chapter 8), demonstrating movement (such as a golf swing), or insuring that you "get the moment." The typical interval between frames is currently about 1.5 frames per second. Faster is better.

Best-shot mode

This feature can be used to insure steadiness and sharp focus. The camera shoots a burst of frames but automatically keeps only the sharpest and/or best-exposed frame.

Movie making

Some cameras can make short (typically 30- to 60-second) movies at a typical rate of 15 frames per second. Because these movies are meant primarily for use on the Web, resolution is generally limited. Some cameras give you a choice of resolutions but generally top out at 640 pixels x 480 pixels.

Sound recording

This feature lets you record short notes about each frame you shoot. If you are using image-management database software (see Chapter 9), you will be able to play back your notes and type them in to that software's information fields. Of course, you can say anything you want.

CHAPTER 2

TAKING YOUR FIRST PICTURE

IN THIS CHAPTER

- Preparing to take your first photo
- Taking your first picture
- Getting accessories for your camera

All you need to take your first picture is your digital camera. If you set the camera up properly, it will be able to make the settings needed to take a passable picture automatically. Of course, this chapter will give you some tips for making your pictures look even better.

Getting Ready to Shoot

Before you go on your first picture-taking quest, you want to look over your camera's manual to make sure that you have properly charged and installed the batteries that power the camera. At least one set of these batteries probably came with the camera.

Next, you want to make sure that the memory needed to store the pictures has been installed. A few of the least expensive digital cameras have all the picture-storing memory permanently built-in, so installing memory won't be a problem. Most digital cameras, however, use a small removable memory card. You want to make sure that you've found it, that it's been properly inserted, and that its protective door has been closed.

If this isn't the first time the camera has been used, you also need to read your camera's manual to discover how to preview the images that may already be on the memory card so that you can decide whether or not to keep them. If you want to keep the previously recorded images, read your manual to discover how to transfer them onto a computer. After you've transferred any images you want to keep, read the instructions that tell how to erase all the pictures on the currently installed memory card.

Several types of memory cards are used in popular digital cameras. Most often, this memory is some form of *solid-state* (no moving parts) *non-volatile* (the information doesn't go away when the power's turned off) storage called *flash memory*. The most popular forms of flash memory cards are called SmartMedia, CompactFlash, and Memory Stick. Some digital cameras even use removable disks (such as floppies or the Imation Super Floppy) instead of flash memory for storing images. Regardless of which of these types of memory your camera uses, you can assume that the advice I give for dealing with image-memory devices will apply unless I point to specific exceptions.

Finally, you want to read the manual to find out how to set the camera in fully automatic mode. Your camera may give you many other setup options, but all digital cameras priced less than $1,500 have an automatic mode.

Okay, so now you're just about ready to go out to take your first pictures. Your camera's batteries are installed and fully charged, and your image storage space is empty and ready for a fresh set of pictures. Be sure to bring your manual along — just in case you need it. You may want to add other accessories as you become more experienced, but you're already equipped for the basics.

Understanding the Basics

Remember that your digital camera knows how to set itself to get a generally acceptable picture of whatever you aim your camera at — unless there's just not enough light. Your camera makes a good guess as to how far away the object in the center of the frame is from the camera and sets its focus accordingly. Finally, it automatically compensates for the color of the prevailing light. All you have to do to make sure that all of this is so, is to follow the instructions in your camera manual that sets the camera in a state that is generally referred to as "fully automatic" or "point-and-shoot" mode.

So if the camera can do all the thinking for you, what do you need to know in order to be able to take good pictures? Here's a quick list:

- How to eliminate distracting elements
- What to leave in and what to leave out
- How to avoid lens flare
- How to control what's in focus
- How to avoid camera movement

Knowing when to use the viewfinder over the LCD

If your subject is more than six feet away, use your camera's *optical viewfinder* (the small window — at the top left of most digital cameras — used to frame shots) that you look through to frame rather than the LCD preview monitor screen. You'll be able to see what's going on in your picture more clearly, and you'll save the life of your batteries. Most LCD preview screens must be powered on to be visible, and this requires significantly more battery power.

Some accessory lenses are so big that they interfere with your ability to see through the viewfinder. If you have this problem, use an LCD hood and your LCD viewfinder.

Making point-and-shoot work

Point-and-shoot is the term used to describe cameras that make all the focusing and exposure settings automatically. Today's digital cameras — especially those that cost more than $350 — have surprisingly accurate built-in light meters. You're most likely to get the right exposure if you follow these steps:

1. Start by centering your subject in the viewfinder.

2. Depress the shutter button partway to activate the exposure meter.

3. Reframe your shot.

4. Finish depressing the shutter button to take the shot.

Eventually, you complete these steps so quickly that the process becomes one smooth motion.

You should keep a few other "rules" in mind. Table 2-1 and Table 2-2 list things you should and shouldn't do when taking pictures with your camera.

Table 2-1:   You Should

You Should	How and Why
Brace yourself	The best lens in the world won't give you a sharp picture if you don't stay still. If you're not using a tripod, at least press the camera tight against your face and squeeze your arms to your body — then take a deep, calm breath and click.
Keep the sun behind the lens	If the sun strikes the lens directly, you'll get a very soft-focus photo with no blacks.

You Should	How and Why
Frame your picture so that it includes no more detail than necessary	Trimming a picture after it's taken in order to eliminate unwanted detail and then enlarging it to the same size as pictures that haven't been trimmed will result in poor definition of fine detail (such as hair or fabric textures). This is especially true if the resolution of your digital camera is less than two megapixels.

Table 2-2:   You Shouldn't

You Shouldn't	Why
Pass up a chance for a happy accident	If you have only one chance to take this picture and the conditions are wrong, take it anyway. It doesn't cost anything, and there's a 1:100 chance that you'll love the results.
Use your camera in bad weather or extreme heat and humidity	You'll get unacceptably blotchy images, poor color fidelity, and risk ruining your camera.
Take a picture from a vibrating platform	Don't photograph from a moving car, bouncing bridge, or galloping horse. You'll get blurry pictures — even in bright light.
Overcompress your pictures	If you use less than the highest definition compression setting, you will lose information in the image you can't replace. If you need to take more pictures before tansferring your pictures to a computer, buy extra memory cards.

Deciding when to use the flash

Digital cameras tend to turn on the flash automatically whenever they sense that the shutter speed needs to drop below one-sixtieth of a second. The manufacturer's theory is that you'd rather have a sharp photo than one that's attractively (and naturally) lit. If you don't agree with the manufacturer

(I seldom do), be sure to turn off your camera's flash as soon as you turn on the camera. On the other hand, here are two times when you definitely should use flash:

- **Whenever it's too dark to get a steady handheld shot.** This may seem to contradict what I said earlier in this chapter about turning the flash off as soon as you turn the camera on, but if you start seeing unacceptably blurry photos on your preview screen, turn the flash on.

- **In very bright direct sunlight.** Otherwise, you'll get solid white highlights with no texture and charcoal-black shadows. This is especially unflattering when you're taking pictures of people. If your camera has a *fill-flash mode* (which automatically sets the flash to provide just enough light to brighten shadows and not overpower the main existing light source), use it. Otherwise, use the flash anyway. The highlight (sunlit) areas of the picture will probably still be brighter anyway.

Accessorizing Your Camera

On the other hand, a few inexpensive accessories and some simple suggestions can help you take pictures that you'll be 1000 percent happier to share with others.

You're faced with two choices when you set out to take your first digital pictures: Take your chances, or be prepared for almost anything. If you're willing to give up on trying to get good shots when there's strong backlight or not enough light, just stick your digital camera in your pocket and go. On the other hand, if you invest in a few small and affordable accessories, you'll be able to avoid some very common problems. Making sure that a few accessories are in your cargo pants or camera bag is a good idea.

Choosing lens caps and keepers

A lens cap is an absolute necessity if you expect your pictures to be as sharp in a few weeks or months as they are when your camera is new. Without a lens cap, your lens is likely to get scratched when it's tumbling around in your bag or pocket. You'd do well to order a couple of extra lens caps when you buy your camera.

Some cameras have a sliding door that covers the lens when the camera is not in use. If you have such a camera, you don't need a lens cap.

Lens caps are easily lost. Go to your local camera store and buy a $5 accessory called a keeper. A *keeper* consists of two strips of adhesive hook-and-loop fasteners, one for the lens cap and one for the camera. The two strips are attached by a cord. If the lens cap falls off accidentally, it will just dangle on the cord. To keep the lens cap from dangling into your shot, you just stick the hook-and-loop fastener on the lens to the hook-and-loop fastener on the camera.

Using a lens shade

A *lens shade* is a device that keeps stray light (even that reflected from white shirts or nearby white walls) from bouncing off the surface of the lens. Stray light on the lens surface causes a loss of picture sharpness and contrast. Lens shades are also good insurance against accidentally scratching your lens when the camera is dangling from a neck strap.

Purchasing a neck strap

Hopefully, your camera comes with a wide, soft, and comfortable neck strap. If not, you can buy one for less than $15. Many cameras have only one place to attach a strap — usually a wrist strap. Pitch the wrist strap — it's useless and can get in the way when you're in a hurry. Buy one of those wire key rings and pass it through the wrist strap loop. Then you can attach both ends of the neck strap to the wire ring. Figure 2-1 depicts a typical neck strap.

Figure 2-1: A typical neck strap.

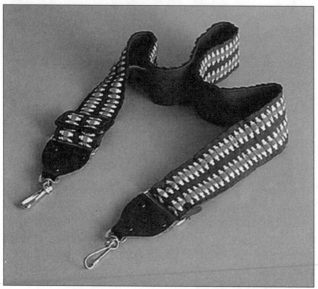

Investing in an LCD hood

If you don't have some means of shading your liquid-crystal preview screen (LCD) from bright light, you won't be able to see it comfortably in outdoor light. Because the camera you own will likely be used outdoors most of the time, that's a big problem. Get an Extend-a-View (as shown in Figure 2-2) or Hoodman accessory that shades the LCD. Then you'll be able to use your LCD preview screen as a viewfinder for close-ups and be able to read your camera's menus whenever you want to change settings or preview the pictures you've taken.

Figure 2-2:   The Photosolve Extend-a-View LCD hood.

Choosing a carrying case or camera bag

You'll want something to carry your camera in so that you can keep the manual and the other accessories with it. The handiest thing I've found is an inexpensive nylon version of the traditional camera bag. Even with all their accessories, modern digital cameras are so small that such bags have plenty of room for my cell phone and palm-sized computer, not to mention spare batteries and flash memory digital film cards.

However, if you're working in crowds or covering an event, the next best thing is a pair of cargo pants — the baggy ones that have six to eight big pockets. You can put everything you need into those pockets and never have to worry about leaving your camera bag on a table where it can be stolen. You won't be snagging a bag on people and posts as you zip through the crowd either.

Getting extra batteries

Whether your camera came with four NiMH rechargeable batteries and a charger or not, get yourself some. (Many cameras come with both.) NiMH rechargeable batteries have twice the life in a digital camera as NiCads, and you can recharge them at any time without having to worry about shortening battery life. A set may cost you close to $50 but will pay for itself in a few shooting sessions.

Just in case you don't have time to recharge your batteries, keep a spare set of fully charged rechargeables handy in your camera bag for when the batteries die.

Investing in memory cards

Most cameras come with ridiculously stingy film cards. Buying another film card so that you can keep taking pictures when you suddenly realize that your card is full is a good idea. Get a film card with the highest capacity (rated in MB or megabytes) you can afford. Then keep the card that came with the camera as a backup. Figure 2-3 shows both Compact Flash and SmartMedia memory cards.

Figure 2-3: CompactFlash (left) and SmartMedia (right) memory cards.

Using different types of flash

Virtually all digital cameras have a built-in flash, so you'll have at least some flash options available to you at all times. However, if you're going to be shooting indoor events or need to be able to control the direction of light in a flash shot, you'll need an external flash that packs more power than that built into the camera. You don't need an external flash connector to make one of these work as long as you're not shooting in bright daylight. You can buy a high-powered unit that houses a flash-firing, light-sensitive cell called a *slave sensor*. The slave sensor causes the external flash to fire at the exact instant that your built-in flash fires.

Selecting a tripod

In dim lighting conditions, your camera will require a slow shutter speed in order to get correct exposure. At these slow shutter speeds, any slight movement of the camera will result in a blurry picture. You must do two things in order to solve this problem:

- Ask your subject to stay still ("hold it, please") — or wait until the subject is naturally motionless.

- Place your camera on a solid base so that it won't move when the shutter button is clicked.

Perhaps the handiest means of keeping your camera steady is a tripod if you're going to shoot static scenery and still-life shots. You'll also need to keep your camera steady if you want to photograph anything by available light indoors or outdoors between dusk and full sunset. You'll also need a tripod if you plan to shoot any multiple-frame panoramas (see Chapter 8). Many digital cameras come with software for making such panoramas.

The most universally adaptable means of keeping the camera steady is a tripod. Digital cameras are so small and light that even the cheapest tripods can be made to work.

You should get a tripod with either a ball head (the camera swings and tilts in any direction when a single adjustment is loosened or tightened) or a more-traditional head that has separate adjustments for swings (from side-to-side) and tilts. Swing and tilt heads are more accurate for shooting panoramas.

If you need to stay portable and don't have the time or room to carry a tripod, you should consider a tabletop tripod or a unipod. Tabletop tripods are miniatures that can be used atop any surface. Unipods have only one leg and can be used as a walking stick.

CHAPTER 3
SHOOTING OUTDOORS

IN THIS CHAPTER

- Taking advantage of the time of day and year
- Balancing light
- Balancing color
- Getting exposure right
- Aperture priority versus shutter priority
- Controlling focus
- Strengthening your message with good composition

This chapter is called "Shooting Outdoors" because this is the circumstance in which you'll most often find yourself taking pictures, primarily because there's usually enough light outdoors to permit photography with a handheld camera and with little or no supplementary lighting. However, you can apply most of what is said in this chapter to shooting indoors, as long as the light indoors is bright enough.

Taking Pictures in Existing Light

The factor that will most influence the overall look of your digital (or conventional) pictures is the quality of the existing light. The quality of light is mostly influenced by the time of day and season that you are taking your pictures. Table 3-1 shows the characteristics of light for different times of the day.

Table 3-1:   Some Characteristics of Light

Time of Day	Quality of Light
Sunrise or sunset	Long, sharp-edged shadows. Light is blue when sun is below the horizon; red when just above.
Midmorning or midafternoon	Safest. Best contrast compromise; best color balance.
Noon	High contrast, shallow shadows, bags under eyes, washed-out skies.

The qualities of light that you should pay attention to are the following:

■ **Direction of light.** This equates to the position of the sun. Generally, you want the sun at your back but not too high in the sky.

■ **Contrast of light.** Lighting with ultrabright highlights and very deep shadows (*contrasty* lighting) can be dramatic, but it generally results in loss of shadow and highlight detail. Soft lighting, where there is only a slight difference between highlights and shadows, results in more-flattering portraits and much more detail in the light and dark portions of the picture.

■ **Color of light.** If the sun is being filtered by clouds or a sunrise or sunset, the *color* balance (overall color tint) of your image may be upset. Sometimes, such changes in tint can be disturbing, but they may also be emotionally appealing. Your image-editing program will allow you to change the color balance after making the shot.

■ **Brightness of light.** The overall intensity of sunlight will determine whether you need to take extra care to steady the camera or use supplementary lighting to brighten shadow areas.

You should keep the following things in mind while you are shooting outdoors:

- **Don't shoot at noon:** When the sun is directly overhead, lighting is unflattering to both people and landscapes. You'll see pale, washed-out faces with eyes that look like dark holes. Especially with digital cameras, highlights tend to lose detail and shadows tend to turn black because the lighting is so contrasty.

- **Don't point at the sun:** Pointing the lens at the sun could damage the image sensor in your digital camera, particularly if it has no mechanical shutter (the type found in conventional film cameras, but seldom in digital cameras). Also, you'll get a phenomenon called *lens flare,* which causes a bright spot to blot out detail or — at the least — causes strange rings in the picture and lowered contrast over all or part of the picture.

- **The best sun angles are midmorning and midafternoon:** At these times of the day, the sun is least likely to cause lens flare. Shadows taper off at about a 45° angle and are just long enough to give definition to the subject. Yet shadows aren't so long that they hide a lot of the detail, particularly if the sun is over one or the other of the photographer's shoulders.

- **Sunrise and sunset are good for drama:** At those times of day, the light takes on a reddish or bluish tint, and the shadows get long and dramatic. These are not particularly good times of day for accurate color and full-range detail, but they are wonderful for conveying mood, emotion, and drama. Sunset is also the one time of the day when a little lens flare from a setting sun can increase the mood. Just before sunrise and just after sunset can also be great times for softly lit and moody (or sexy) portraits and scenes with people in them — but you'll probably need to bring along a tripod. For the most part, don't use flash at this time of day. It won't match the color of the prevailing light and will destroy the natural direction of the shadows.

■ **Shadows are longer and lighting less harsh in winter:** Winter light, especially for landscapes, can be lovely. Skies tend to be more dramatic, and lighting is softer and moodier (usually bluer). You also get nice long dramatic shadows, but without the harsh contrast that's more likely in spring and summer when there's less atmospheric haze to diffuse the sun.

Shooting Pictures When the Light Isn't Ideal

After appraising the quality of light at different times of the day, you realize that lighting is likely to be less than ideal at most times of the day. So what do you do when you have to shoot under less-than-ideal conditions? The answer is to find ways to balance the light. Here are easy and affordable ways to do that if you have a point-and-shoot camera:

■ **Watching the clouds and sky:** The best days to shoot are those with lots of clouds. Clouds diffuse the sunlight. The result is less glare in the highlights and brighter, more-detailed shadows. Of course, if no clouds are covering (or partly covering) the sun, this won't be true. Still, if the sky has lots of clouds, all you have to do is wait a few minutes for the lighting to change.

■ **Overcast days:** Completely overcast days are great for shooting close-ups of people and things because the very soft light means that all the shades of color in the scene are likely to be recorded was taken on a completely cloudy day. Note the full range of detail in both highlights and shadows.

Figure 3-1: Photo taken on an overcast day.

■ **Lightening shadows with fill flash:** When the lighting conditions are such that there is too great a difference in the brightness of highlights and shadows to record the detail in both, the easiest cure is fill flash (that is, if your camera has a fill-flash mode — you'll have to check your manual). If your camera does have a fill-flash mode, it automatically sets the brightness of the flash to be less than the brightness of the light in the highlighted areas of the picture — thus assuring that the existing light will still have the main influence over the direction and edge-sharpness of shadows. Use fill flash when the sun is very bright and direct or when it's behind your subject (thus throwing the important details into shadow).

Various cameras are different in their capabilities to calculate a desirable ratio of brightness between highlights and shadows. If your foregrounds are brighter than your backgrounds when you use fill flash, turn it off.

- **Using reflectors:** One of the easiest and most attractive ways to balance shadows and highlights is to use a reflector to throw light into the shadow areas of the images. Snapshooters don't use them more often for two reasons: Someone needs to hold the reflector, and reflectors can be bulky and hard to tote.

Tip

The best reflector is a piece of white foamcore mounting board (about $5 at any office or art supply store). The most commonly available size is the 32" x 40" inches. Cut the board into 10-inch-wide strips; then hinge the strips together with white tape. (The tape needs to be as white as the board so that the surface will stay evenly reflective.) Now you have a cheap, lightweight, and transportable reflector. Someone still needs to hold it, but if you put your camera on a tripod, that person could be you. Place the reflector on opposite side of the subject from the sun and then angle the reflector so that it reflects light back onto the shadow side of the subject. You can get farther away from the camera (and have more control over the distance and angle of the reflector) if your camera has a remote control or self-timer. Or just take along a friend or pay an assistant to hold the reflector for you.

- **Getting into the shade:** If you're shooting people or portable objects, you can eliminate the high-contrast-lighting problem by moving your subjects under a tree, under an umbrella, or into the shade of a building. Try to avoid shade provided by translucent glass or fabric that may significantly change the color of the light falling on the subject.

Balancing Color

Balancing color (sometimes called *white balancing*) is the act of correcting the overall tint of color that would occur when shooting in light that isn't the same color as pure daylight. If you don't make any adjustments to the contrary, most digital cameras will do this automatically. There's also a very good chance that you can adjust your camera specifically for daylight, tungsten, or fluorescent light. Those options can be useful because your camera automatically corrects for color tints by applying a formula to the average color of the light that it sees reflected in whatever scene it's pointed at. If the subject itself is too much of one prevailing color, however, the camera could make a very bad guess as to the correct color balance.

You can do a lot of color balancing in even the most basic of image-editing programs, so you don't need to be overly concerned with small changes in the prevalent color of light. Preview the first picture you've taken in an unusual lighting situation on your LCD.

Getting the Right Exposure

Exposure is the process of controlling the amount of light that strikes the "film" (or, in the case of a digital camera, the light-sensitive image capture cell). If you have too much light, your picture will appear washed out. Too little light, and your picture appears dark and muddy. Most of the time, getting the right exposure to capture as many tones in the image as possible is automatic, but you can choose the area of the picture that you want to set the exposure for:

1. If you have a zoom lens, zoom in to frame the shot as you wish.

2. Aim the camera so that the most important area of the picture is dead center. Forget about framing for the moment.

3. Press the shutter button partway (approximately halfway) down. The camera will automatically set exposure, white balance, and focus. Don't change the pressure of your finger on the shutter button. Performing this step will lock the automatic settings until you actually take the picture.

4. If necessary, move the camera to frame the picture as you'd like.

5. Press the shutter button further to take the picture.

Some cameras have a feature called something like "spot metering mode" (see "Using spot metering mode," later in this chapter). If your camera has this feature, you can have even more control over which area of the picture is most important because the camera will take into account only a tiny circle in the very center of the picture.

Making multiple exposures of the same subject

Remember that in digital photography, film and processing cost nothing. If your camera lets you change the exposure increment (shown as a + or - value), take the first picture of a scene three times, one at the automatic setting (0) and one each at -1 and +1. Then preview the results on your LCD. Take the rest of your shots of that subject from that location and point of view at that setting. The lovely thing about working this way is that you'll always get the right exposure for the mood you want to set and for the tonal values in your subject. Of course, this technique is useless for action shooting. You can, however, take three different exposures of the scene, preview them on your camera's LCD monitor and then, when you take your action shots, use the same exposure setting as that used for the shot you liked best.

Using spot metering mode

As I noted earlier in this chapter, many digital cameras have a mode called *spot metering mode*. In this mode, the camera judges exposure only by what it sees inside a very small circle at the very center of the image. Spot metering is very useful when the exposure of a particular part of a scene is of critical importance. First, you set your camera for spot metering. (The method differs from camera to camera.) Then you aim your camera so that the critical area is vertically and horizontally centered in your viewfinder, depress the shutter button partway, reframe your shot, and continue depressing the shutter to take the picture. Figure 3-2 shows the spot metering zone in a typical digital camera viewfinder.

Figure 3-2: The circle in the center is the spot metering zone.

Using cameras that enable you to choose exposure

A few of the newer and more advanced digital cameras let you choose exposures for certain types of shooting situations, such as sports, snowscapes, or sunsets. If your camera has this feature, use it.

Considering Aperture Priority versus Shutter Priority

Some cameras let you choose between exposure modes called aperture priority and shutter priority. Aperture priority mode is appropriate when you want to control depth of field. If you choose *aperture priority*, you can set a specific *aperture* (lens opening or f-stop), and the camera automatically chooses the correct shutter speed. The smaller the aperture you choose, the greater the *depth of field* (distance between the nearest and farthest objects that are in sharp focus). A larger f-stop number indicates a smaller aperture.

If you choose *shutter priority*, you can set a specific shutter speed, and the camera automatically chooses the correct aperture. This mode is appropriate when you want to intentionally freeze or blur moving subjects or to make sure that you get a steady shot.

Controlling Focus

The reason photographers want to control depth of field is to keep the viewer focused on the center of interest and to minimize confusing background detail. However, most digital cameras have nearly infinite depth of field.

Another aspect of controlling the appearance of your images is the capability to control focus. With most digital cameras, that capability is minimal (due to technical factors beyond the scope of this book). Everything from about eight feet to infinity tends to be in sharp focus, even at the widest aperture. The best way to control focus is in on your computer after the shot has been downloaded from the camera. You would use software meant for editing (altering) digital (or conventional converted to digital) photographs. (See Chapter 6 for information about editing photographs.)

Some cameras have the ability to shoot extreme close-ups. This is called a *macro capability*. In macro mode, for technical reasons beyond the scope of this book, focus becomes more critical. Be sure to center your subject, depress the shutter part way to set the focus, frame your picture, and finish depressing the shutter to shoot.

Using Composition to Add Impact

What you decide to include and to leave out of your pictures, all other considerations being equal, will make or break them. The first rule is this: Don't be afraid to move in close. Be sure to leave out anything that doesn't contribute to the statement you want your picture to make. Also, leave out anything that should be a subject unto itself. In other words, don't put your kids and the Grand Canyon in the same photo.

Beyond that, a few rules of composition tend to work more often than not.

The *image definition* of currently available *prosumer* (serious or professional consumer) to consumer-level digital cameras (that is, priced under $1,000) is one-half to one-fourth that of medium-speed 35mm film. As a result, there's not enough *definition* (resolution, image quality) to make it permissible to throw away a large portion of the image. This makes careful framing (*composition*) of the in-camera image much more important in point-and-shoot digital photography than in conventional photography.

Rule of thirds

Given that digital cameras make it so much more important to compose a shot in the camera (rather than after-the-fact on the computer), you would do well to understand the most basic rule of good composition: The rule of thirds. The simplest way to state the rule of thirds is that you shouldn't place the center of interest in the center of the picture. Imagine dividing the picture into a grid of nine equal cells — three across and three down. The composition will almost always be stronger if the center of interest is placed at one of the grid intersections and if strong lines (formed by the edges of objects in the picture) fall between the horizontal or vertical grid lines.

Direction of implied movement

Even a static photograph of a person, car, animal, or of many other momentarily still subjects has an implied direction of movement. That is to say that people, animals, and vehicles are expected to move forward. You want to have the subject's direction of implied movement facing into the picture, not trapped by the edge of the picture.

CHAPTER 4
SHOOTING INDOORS

IN THIS CHAPTER

- Shooting in dimmer light
- Balancing indoor/outdoor light
- Using light meters for indoor and studio work
- Using steady lighting
- Using flash
- Lighting portraits and products

What You Need to Know about Shooting in Low Light

One of the first problems with shooting indoors is that the brightness of the lighting drops to a fraction of what it is in daylight (except, of course, near or after sunset/sunrise). Furthermore, the scene is likely to be lit by artificial lighting, which can vary a great deal in color. This means that, if you want to shoot while using the existing indoor lighting, you need to:

- Brace the camera with a tripod or other device (see Chapter 2) because the shutter speed will drop.

- Predetermine, if possible, whether the color balance is set for daylight, *tungsten* (most light bulbs with a filament), or fluorescent lighting.

- Choose a higher-than-normal ISO rating if you can.

Many of the things you learned about shooting outdoors apply equally to shooting indoors — especially the use of tripods and other camera-steadying devices and the use of external flash.

Balancing Indoor/Outdoor Light

If you're shooting indoors but are near windows, you are faced with two problems:

■ The light outside is usually much brighter than the light inside.

■ The light outside is very blue, provided mostly by sky light (about 6,000° Kelvin), while the light from inside — usually from tungsten or fluorescent bulbs — is reddish-yellow (roughly 3,400° Kelvin).

The easy way to solve both problems is to let your camera automatically choose to use its flash. If you're shooting a birthday party or your friend's visit, this approach does the job. You will be limited to subjects that are six to twelve feet from your camera. Also, there is a strong rim of shadow that outlines the subject. Finally, light falls away very quickly, resulting in dark backgrounds.

Using Light Meters for Indoor and Studio Work

A *light meter* is an instrument that measures light and then indicates how to set the camera's lens aperture (f-stop) and shutter speed in order to record an image in which the most important areas of the subject are of the desired brightness. The two basic types of light meters are the following:

■ **Incident light meters:** These measure light falling on the subject.

■ **Reflected light meters:** These measure light reflected from the subject.

Most point-and-shoot digital cameras limit you to using the camera's built-in light meter, which can be used to make the *exposure* (aperture and shutter speed) settings automatically.

However, by using the two-stage shutter depression method (partway to set focus and exposure, fully depressed to take the picture), you can exert extra control over your exposure. Figure 4-1 shows a photo taken by making a spot reading from one of the faces, so that the light coming from the window doesn't cause the rest of the picture to go dark.

Figure 4-1:   Exposure was based entirely on the skin tones in one of the faces.

If you have strong light coming through a window but your subject is lit mainly by the interior light, follow these simple steps:

1. First, take your reading with the camera pointed away from the window. Preferably, take the reading from a medium-gray card or the face of someone off-camera.

2. Next, partially depress your shutter. Because depressing the shutter part way also sets the focus, make sure that the surface you take your reading from is approximately the same distance away from you as your subject is.

3. After you've depressed the shutter partway to lock in the exposure and focus, swing the camera to frame the subject as you'd like and press harder to take the shot.

An even better option is to use a spot metering mode, if your camera's meter is so equipped. Aim the center of the viewfinder frame at the area you want properly exposed (typically, someone's face), press the shutter half way, frame your shot, and continue depressing the shutter to take the photo.

If your camera lets you set exposure manually, you can use an external incident light meter. If you use flash, you may want the variety that can read both continuous and electronic flash lighting. Two companies that make such meters are Gossen and Sekonic. The meters start at about $250 and can go way up from there. Incident light meters read the average of the light falling on the face of the subject. The advantage is that they aren't influenced by the lightness or brightness of the scene itself, so the scene is more likely to be recorded at its original brightness.

Using Incandescent Lighting

Incandescent lighting is any lighting driven by electricity. Unlike the sun, you can easily reposition most incandescent lighting (except, of course, ceiling lights) so that you can control the direction and intensity of light. However, incandescent lighting is seldom as bright as natural outdoor light, and it has a different overall color. The exact color of a given incandescent light source is usually measured in degrees Kelvin and is referred to as *color temperature*. Incandescent lights generally fall into one of two categories: tungsten and fluorescent. Tungsten lights are generally meant to include any light bulb that includes a metal filament, even if that filament isn't really tungsten. Fluorescent lights are gas-filled tubes.

Household and workplace lamps

Household and workplace lamps tend to be a bit warmer in color than the incandescent bulbs typically used for photo lighting. If you need to position and direct light, you can buy inexpensive reflectors (bowl-shaped brushed or polished metal with a screw-in lamp receptacle in the center), clamps, and lamp stands; and you can use extra bright bulbs in all the fixtures. Doing all this will help to shorten exposures by bringing up the overall level of light. This may be worth doing if you want a natural-lighting look for rooms that you're photographing (for example) for a real-estate site.

Fluorescent

Fluorescent lighting can present a problem because most fluorescent bulbs put out peak light at two different color temperatures, which typically gives a sickly green cast to skin tones and highlights. Some digital cameras have a fluorescent white balance setting, which helps as long as the fluorescent isn't mixed with tungsten or daylight in the same picture. If it is, the best cure is to go to a photo lighting supply house and purchase rolls of a clear plastic that converts the tungsten light to daylight. Some special tungsten bulbs are made to match daylight, and you could substitute those bulbs. However, you'll probably want to save these last solutions for critical jobs and rely on being able to balance color in your image editor.

Inexpensive tungsten photo gear

If you want to light an interior with the same color of light as that coming through the windows, you can buy blue-coated tungsten bulbs and substitute them for the existing bulbs. These blue-coated bulbs typically cost $4 to $10 each and also come in 500- to 1000-watt versions that shouldn't be used in most household fixtures. You can, however, use these high-wattage bulbs in studio-type bowl reflectors on tripod-based light stands. A reflector and stand will cost between $25 and $100 — depending on type and quality. In addition to being affordable, these units are lightweight and easily portable. These characteristics make them excellent for shooting portraits, still lifes, and product shots on location.

Using External Flash

The flash that is built into your camera may make taking a picture possible when there would otherwise not be enough light. However, built-in flash almost always looks amateurish and rarely flatters the subject of the picture. Highlights tend to be too bright, *red eye* (light reflected back from the retina of the subject's eyes, causing the pupils to glow red) is a problem, and harsh shadows appear under the chin, nose, and eyebrows. Often, the subject's shadow is cast on the wall behind him or her. If you can use external flash, you will have much more control over the direction and quality of light. Also, external flash is almost always brighter than the tiny units built into cameras; as a result, external flash units can cover a much broader area, and subjects can be much farther from the camera.

You have the option of using external flash, even if your camera doesn't have a connection for external flash. All you need is a *slave trigger* (see "Slave flashes and triggers," later in this chapter). Having an industry-standard, external-flash connector, however, also gives you the following advantages:

- You can use all types of industry-standard flash units, both portable and electronic flash.

- You can use the external flash while your built-in flash is disabled, so you don't get any more fill than is necessary.

- You can use the external flash outdoors.

The primary advantage of external flash is that it can cover a much greater distance than the built-in flash. An external flash may also be bright enough to allow you to use smaller apertures, giving you greater depth -of field. A handheld external flash unit is shown in Figure 4-2.

Figure 4-2:   An external flash unit with a built-in slave unit

Determining exposure for external flash

Of course, you must be able to determine the brightness of any light source that you're using for photography in order to make a correct exposure. Several ways of determining exposure for external flash are available. Table 4-1 lists each method and its pros and cons. An external flash that has variable power settings (most do, but check to be sure) best assures you that you will be able to get the correct exposure. Remember that some cameras can set their exposure only automatically.

Table 4-1: Ways to Determine Proper Flash Exposure

Method	Pros and Cons
Make a test shot	This method provides the best assurance you have the correct exposure, and it costs nothing because your test shot can be erased. You can move flash nearer to or farther from the subject to compensate — or change the power setting on the flash. This procedure is not spontaneous, so you have to test before the critical moment comes.
Use a guide number	Most portable electronic flash units have a wheel on the top that lets you calculate the exposure based on the distance from the light to the subject divided into the electronic flash's guide number. You then change the electronic flash's power settings or the camera's aperture to compensate.
Use a flash meter	Hold the meter directly in front of the subject, press its button, fire the flash, and set the camera according to the readout on the meter. Fast and highly accurate. Prices start at around $250. This method requires a camera that permits aperture priority or manual setting of f-stop.

Portable electronic flash

Portable electronic flash units are those that are battery-powered and generally small enough to fit into a camera bag. Prices depend on power and features, but most units are between $80 and $250, with the most bang-for-the-buck in the middle of that price range.

Studio electronic flash

These units start at around $250 and go into the stratosphere. They almost always require a light stand. If you're shooting lots of products or formal portraits, these units will give you the power to stop action at small apertures and the ability to use several lamp heads; these units are also adaptable to a wide variety of accessories and reflectors. This category of electronic flashes is best matched to higher-end digital cameras with provision for external flash synch and manual exposure settings.

Slave flashes and triggers

A *slave trigger* is simply a photosensitive cell that plugs into the synchronization connector on your flash unit. When a slave trigger sees the flash of light from your built-in flash, it causes the external unit to fire in perfect synchronization. You can buy these slave triggers for virtually every type of flash unit. However, some digital cameras fire their flash twice: once to take an exposure reading, and a second time to take the picture. Those cameras require a special slave trigger that waits until it sees the second flash. Photosensitive slave triggers cost anywhere from $25 to $100.

If you have a connection for external flash, you can also use a radio or infrared slave. These more-costly units have to consist of a transmitter and a receiver, and the receiver must be connected to the camera's PC or hot shoe connector. The advantage of such slave units is that you can synchronize flashes in daylight and in venues where lots of other photographers are working with flash.

Some digital cameras fire the flash two times in order to set white balance. This double flash has nothing to do with red-eye reduction — which can be turned off in most cameras. These preflash cameras must use a slave flash or flash slave trigger that is especially engineered to fire only on the final flash. You can find out more about such units at www.srelectronics.com.

Lighting Portraits and Products

When you are shooting formal portraits and products, you generally want to have precise control over the quality, direction, and intensity of lighting. This is especially true if your use for digital photography requires consistent results, as would be the case for photographing products for a Web site, portraits for employee or member records, or commercial illustration for almost anything.

Incandescent versus electronic flash lighting

Your budget will probably determine whether you choose to light your subjects with flash (electronic flash) or a constant (incandescent) light source. Even high-output, photo-quality tungsten lighting is much less expensive than the typical studio electronic-flash setup. Check out the pros and cons of each type of lighting, as shown in Table 4-2 and Table 4-3:

Table 4-2: Incandescent Lighting

Advantages	Disadvantages
One-third to one-fifth the cost of studio electronic flashes.	Heat.
What you see is what you get. Easy to study the location and quality of highlights and shadows.	People and animals squint and blink.
Lower light intensity makesshallow focus easier to achieve when shallow depth of field is desirable.	High utility bills.
Lights can be moved during exposure — so you can paint with light.	Bulbs need frequent replacement.
	Slow shutter speeds require subject to freeze.

Table 4-3:   Electronic Flash Lighting

Advantages	Disadvantages
Freezes all but extremely rapid action.	Difficult to use with most low-cost cameras or cameras with no synch.
Easy on the subject's eye.	May be difficult to see modeling lights if ambient light level is too high.
Typically small apertures (f-8 to f-22) tend to keep everything in focus.	
Comfortable operating temperatures.	

If the area you need to photograph is fairly small — such as a head-and-shoulders portrait or a gallon of milk — you can get away with using two or three small portable electronic flash units (and possibly some white foamcore reflectors). At about $100 per unit for each portable flash, this setup wouldn't be a much more expensive than using tungsten light.

The most trustworthy arrangement of lights

All photographic lighting consists of three main sources. They are:

- **Keylight:** This is the light that provides the main highlights in the image and that lights the most important areas of the subject. Generally, you want to expose for the surfaces lit by the keylight.

- **Fill:** This illuminates the shadows cast by the keylight. The fill light is typically about 70 percent as bright as the keylight. However, drama and form will be most influenced by the lightness or darkness of shadow areas.

■ **Backlight:** This is used to illuminate the silhouette of the subject. Backlight is often supplied by light reflected from walls. It tends to formalize portraits. Backlight can also add depth and help to separate the subject from the background. Use backlight with care, though. When overdone, it looks artificial.

Of course, you can supply all of these light sources with one keylight and carefully placed reflectors. However, doing that successfully in all situations may prove to be an unsolvable challenge.

Any placement of lights may work for a given subject. However, the arrangement that's most successful more often than any other is the one diagrammed in Figure 4-3.

Figure 4-3: A lighting setup that works well for most situations.

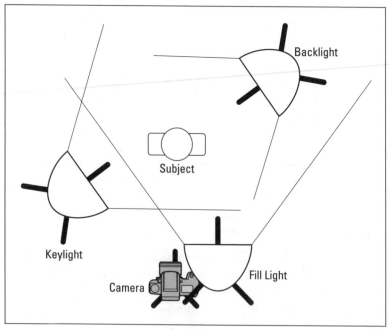

CHAPTER 5

TRANSFERRING YOUR PHOTOS TO A PC

IN THIS CHAPTER

- Getting your computer ready for digital photos
- Adding items to your PC
- Transferring photo files to a PC
- Understanding image file formats

If you leave your photos inside the camera, they won't do you much good at all. In order to place them on a Web site, e-mail them to friends and family, or make prints, you need to transfer them from the camera to your computer. You have two ways that you can do this: either directly from the camera via a cable or by removing the *digital film card* (the removable memory device that holds the pictures) from the camera and placing it into a card reader. Both work equally well, but the latter is much faster.

This chapter helps you determine whether your computer equipment is ready to hold, display, and print your photographs; it also provides instructions for transferring the photos to your computer.

Making Sure That Your Computer Is Ready

Before you start transferring your digital photographs to your computer, you need to make sure that you have enough storage space and memory to hold your photographs and display them properly. The following sections explain what you will need.

The amount of disk space you need

Before you start downloading your pictures to your computer, make sure that you have plenty of storage space on your hard drive. The average digital image, in the JPEG format used by the camera to store images, uses 1MB (megabyte) to 3MB of hard-drive storage. Your average camera card contains 8MB worth of images, JPEG compressed to about 25 percent of their actual size. If you download one card a week and decompress all the images, that's 1.6GB (gigabytes) a year. You also need to remember that you're likely to make new files derived from the originals as you start using your image-editing software. Those new files will use approximately five times as much space because you should decompress the camera files before modifying them.

At a bare minimum, you should have one free gigabyte of hard-drive space devoted to downloading and editing images and some means of archiving files to some sort of removable storage media (see "Removable storage," later in this chapter).

The amount of memory you need

If your computer meets the system requirements for your image-editing software (listed in the manual or software box), your computer has enough system memory to work with your digital camera as well. Of course, if you want to start with a simple image-editing program, such as the one that came with your digital camera, you'll probably have very low *RAM* (internal volatile system memory) requirements. If you move up to Photoshop 5.5, the RAM requirement jumps up to 64MB minimum. The general rule is that you should have three times as much RAM as the largest file you want to manipulate. Most image-processing programs can substitute hard-drive space for RAM, but this substitution slows all image-editing operations significantly.

The type of display system you need

If you're going to work on color photographs on your computer, you want the computer to be able to display a full range of color. You are assured that this will be the case if your *display system* (monitor and video card) is said to be capable of displaying *24-bit color* (also known as *true color*). These terms are interchangeable and mean that the system is able to display as many colors as the human eye can see. In computers-speak, a shade of a color is as distinct a color as an entirely different color. True color can display 16.8 million colors.

Buying Worthwhile Additions for Your Computer

Certain accessories for your PC can help a great deal when working with digital photos. Of course, different folks will differ in their needs for these. In order of likely importance, these accessories are: removable storage, a color printer, a digitizing pad, extra system memory, and a wide-band Internet connection. I've described the benefits of each of these in the following sections.

Removable storage

Pictures can fill a hard drive faster than anything but video footage. You can easily solve this storage problem by purchasing a CD-ROM recorder. CD-ROMs can be easily written, so that your pictures can be read by most Windows-based, Mac OS-based, and UNIX-based computers. CD-ROMs are much less susceptible to damage or accidental erasure than hard drives are. Finally, the CD-ROM discs are less than $1.50 each. You may also find a removable hard drive, such as a Zip or Jaz drive, handy for storing files until you're ready to transfer them to CD-ROM.

Color printer

Most folks who use a digital camera want to be able to print their photos so that they can share them with friends or show them to clients. The good news is that some of the very best printers for making color photos — color inkjet printers — are among the least expensive printers available. You can buy a color inkjet printer capable of turning out acceptable color photos for as little as $89, although $250 is closer to the price typically paid for true photo-quality letter-size inkjet printers. You should be aware that the inkjet printers with the best reputations as business printers are not usually the same as those with the best reputation for making color photo prints. The best inkjet printers for printing photos use six colors of ink, have very high dots-per-inch counts (1200 to 1400 dpi), and print microscopic (3 to 6 picoliter) dots.

Tip

The paper you use for printing is the most important factor in determining the quality of your printed photos. Following the recommendation of your printer manufacturer for a photo-quality glossy paper is best.

Digitizing pad

If you're going to get serious about image editing and plan to spend much time doing it, you'll want a means of moving the cursor that's much quicker and more accurate than using a mouse. The answer is a digitizing pad (as shown in Figure 5-1). A *digitizing pad* is a tablet that tracks the movement of a pen just as though it were drawing on paper. Using a digitizing pad is much more accurate than using a mouse and wielding a pen feels much more natural than pushing around a mouse. The best digitizing pads are those that have a pressure-sensitive pen that doesn't require batteries. *Pressure sensitivity* means that you can vary the thickness or opacity of strokes according to how hard you press. Batteryless pens don't become erratic when the batteries fade and are the same weight and size as ordinary pens.

Figure 5-1:   A digitizing pad and pen.

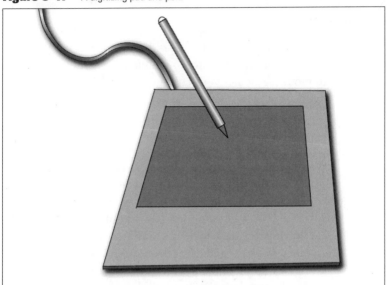

Memory

As you start to increase the complexity of your image editing or increase the size of your images or use the computer
to add special effects, you'll find that additional memory can
do more to speed up operations than any other single factor.
Although you can't have too much memory for image editing, the general rule is to have three times as much memory
as the file size of the largest image size that you regularly
manipulate. You can buy additional memory for your computer from almost any source that sells computer supplies.

Wide-band Internet connection

If you need to communicate your images to clients, editors, or
groups of friends, you'll find that the speed of your Internet
connection can make all the difference. A *DSL* (Digital Sub-
scriber Line) or cable connection can increase the speed of
communicating your pictures ten times faster than the typical
dial-up connection.

Transferring the Photo Files to Your Computer

The download instructions for digital cameras vary considerably from manufacturer to manufacturer and from model to model. Whether your computer is a Mac or a PC doesn't matter — the procedure is identical. You'll need to read your camera's manual to get the instructions. However, the following two possibilities apply to almost all digital cameras:

■ **Downloading directly from the camera:** This is the "no extra cost" method. Direct download involves connecting the camera to the computer with either a serial cable or a *USB* (Universal Serial Bus) cable, installing download software (which is usually part of an entry-level image editor), and using the downloaded software to tell the camera to move the images from camera to computer in the form of JPEG (and, in the case of more-advanced cameras, TIFF) image files. These image files can be read by virtually any image-editing program on any type of computer.

■ **Using a separate card reader:** A card reader is a small accessory about the size and shape of a mouse (the computer kind). It has a slot (or slots) in one end to accommodate one or more types of flash memory card. After making sure that you've bought a card reader that's compatible with your flash memory card (some models from Lexar and Microtek are compatible with all types), you insert the card in the reader, and your computer sees the reader as an extra disk drive. At that point, transferring the files is no different than moving any other type of files from one drive to another.

Most of us buy a digital camera assuming that we'll upload images to the computer by using the serial cable included with most digital cameras. Generally, this turns out to be our biggest disappointment about digital photography. This situation is especially true if you own the higher-capacity memory cards and/or one of the newest generations of three to four *megapixel* (millions of pixels per image) cameras. A typical 8MB memory card can take up to half an hour to download from the camera via a serial cable.

You can cut that time down to only a few minutes if your camera has a USB (Universal Serial Bus) connection — a development you'll find only on recent generations of the more-costly consumer digital cameras.

If you want to cut the download time to a minimum, consider buying an external card reader (as shown in Figure 5-2). These devices are about the size of a deck of cards and cost between $50 and $100.

Figure 5-2:   Various types of card readers.

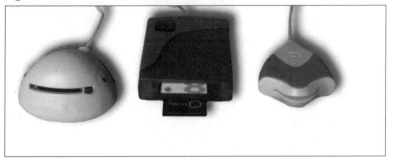

You can buy external card readers that will read both CompactFlash and SmartMedia cards (refer to Figure 2-3 in Chapter 2). Card readers that can read both types of cards are a good investment if you think that you may add a new or different camera in the near future or if several of your colleagues or clients own digital cameras that use another type of digital film card than the one used by your camera.

Understanding the Use of Image File Formats

In order to be able to use picture files in your image-processing program (and when you share them with other computer users or post them on the Web), you will need to understand a little bit about graphics file types.

No single standard exists for organizing picture data in a computer file. The existing standards are called "file types," and, in fact, hordes of file types are around. In order for any of the image-editing programs on your computer to be able to open and edit a photograph, that photograph must first be stored in format that is compatible with that image editor. This could be a major headache, but you are likely to encounter only a few file formats over and over again: *JPEG* (for Joint Photographic Experts Group), *GIF* (Graphics Interchange Format), *TIF* (Tagged Image File), and *PSD* (Photoshop Data). Understanding the specific purpose for each of these file formats pays off in the long run.

If you are a Macintosh user, you'll find that it pays to add the file type extension (a period — or *dot*, as it's called in computerese — followed by the three-letter abbreviation for the file type) to the name of the file. If you add file type extensions, users of other types of computers will be able to read your files. Also, you can identify the type of file by its name. Your image-editing program may provide an option for adding file type extensions automatically.

JPEG

JPEG is the file format that most digital cameras use to store their pictures. The cameras use this format because it uses a computer formula to squeeze an image down to a fraction of its original size, so that more images can be stored onboard the camera before they need to be downloaded to the computer. This technique is known in computerese as *lossy compression* because some image detail is lost in the process of making the image file smaller. Most digital cameras give you a choice of compression levels. Usually these levels are called *quality settings*.

JPEG is also the file format nearly always used for displaying continuous-tone images (as in photographs) on Web pages and for e-mail.

You should always use the highest quality settings your camera allows. Remember that you can never replace image quality that is lost as a result of too much compression. What may seem a reasonable amount of compression now may look completely unacceptable as your equipment and the technology improve or as you become a more sophisticated digital photographer.

GIF

GIF is a very popular Web file format that is unsuitable (except in rare conditions) for photographs because it can display only 256 (or fewer) colors. It is best used for graphics that have geometric hard edges and solid colors, such as buttons, logos, diagrams, and text.

TIF

TIF (or, more formally, TIFF for Tagged Image File Format) is the most popular *lossless* (meaning that none of the original image information is lost) true-color graphics file format that is readable by virtually every graphics program on every type of computer. If you're lucky (and have spent enough money), your camera may give you the option to store files in this format. Using TIF is definitely your best assurance of quality. However, you will be able to store only 2 to 5 pictures (depending on your camera's resolution) on the 8MB digital card that is included in the purchase of most digital cameras.

You should always store files that you are editing in a lossless format such as TIF or PSD (described in the following section). If you use JPEG, you will lose additional image information each time the file is resaved.

PSD (Photoshop)

No consumer-priced digital camera gives you the option to store files in Photoshop format. However, this is the format most frequently used to transfer in-progress image-editing files between computers that use different operating systems or between different image-editing applications. This is because PSD is the file format that allows for multiple layers and masks. (To find out more about layers and masks, see Chapter 6.)

CHAPTER 6
FIXING YOUR PHOTOS DIGITALLY

IN THIS CHAPTER

- Image-processing software

- Killing compression artifacts

- Fixing color balance problems

- Correcting for bad exposure

- Eliminating red eye

- Changing size and proportions

- Exposure compensation

- Getting rid of the unsightly

You can have much more control over the appearance of your photos if you shoot digitally than if you use a point-and-shoot film camera, assuming that you own a computer. You don't need to spend hours getting accustomed to advanced image-processing software, such as Adobe Photoshop, either. Quite a few capable programs, such as Adobe PhotoDeluxe and Kai's PhotoSoap, are in the $50 range. You can learn to use them in an evening. Be careful though — they're so much fun, they're addictive.

This chapter tells you all about image-processing software that is affordable and easy to use. You find out what you can expect from the software that typically comes with your digital camera. You also learn to use the most frequently needed features in Adobe PhotoDeluxe Home Edition, the top-selling, entry-level image-processing software.

What Image-Processing Software Can Do for You

Image-processing software is the digital equivalent of the dark and stinky labs that traditional photographers use to develop film and process prints. This software comes in many price ranges, personalities, and capabilities.

You should expect all image-processing software, regardless of price, to be able to do at least basic *exposure* (brightness and contrast) and *color* (white balance) correction, trim away unwanted portions of the image, resize the image, be able to rotate and flip the image, and automatically correct some common problems, such as the removal of dust, scratches, artifacts, and red eye.

When considering the purchase of entry-level image-processing software, look for a program that is compatible with Photoshop plug-ins (most are). Many such plug-ins are available on the Internet as freeware or shareware.

Using Your Camera's Bundled Software

Most digital cameras include basic downloading and image-editing software, although you may also get a more advanced product as well.

The most important thing the bundled software does is make it easy to download your images directly from your camera, thus eliminating the need for a *card reader* (a device that can read the digital camera's removable memory card or "digital film"). Another function that the bundled software performs is giving you a visual catalog of all the images that have been stored on the camera or on your computer's hard drive.

Working with PhotoDeluxe Image-Processing Software

PhotoDeluxe is typical of entry-level image-processing software in that it requires little to no experience of the user. The user interface almost teaches you the logical sequences involved in image editing by guiding you through a series of operational categories:

■ **Get & Fix Photo.** These are the operations for repairing and otherwise changing the appearance of your photos. In other words, the digital lab operations.

■ **Cards & More.** These operations publish your photos as greeting cards, calendars, pages and certificates, and labels; these operations also create framed photos, make e-mailable slide shows, save and e-mail your photos, or simply print the photos on your printer.

■ **Connectables.** These hook you to sites that offer programs that offer additional capabilities and that are designed to work in PhotoDeluxe.

Clicking the name of each of these operational categories takes you to a screen that coaches you through a sequence of operations. Figure 6-1 shows you the screen for the Get & Fix Photo operations.

If you look at Figure 6-1, you can see how easy it is to use this program. You just take one thing at a time, moving from left to right across the buttons for each of the three modes. Click one of the buttons and you'll find a subset of buttons. Follow each of those from left to right and you'll get the job done — at least as to the essentials.

Figure 6-1: The Get & Fix Photo mode of PhotoDeluxe 3.0 Home Edition.

You can also do much more sophisticated image editing in PhotoDeluxe than the basic, introductory interface might lead you to believe. Click the Advanced Menus button, for example, and you get menus and tools that act very much like Adobe Photoshop (the overwhelming leader in professional-level image editing).

The balance of this chapter shows you how to correct the most common flaws of digital photos. Before getting into that, though, I tell you how to open a program and load a file.

Downloading Photos from Your Camera to Your Computer

Here's how you typically use the bundled software to download images from your camera. This example uses Olympus CAMEDIA, but the software for your own camera will be very similar.

1. Turn off both your computer and your camera (unless you have a USB connection, which allows for very fast image transfer and doesn't require turning off the computer before connecting devices).

2. Attach either the serial cable or USB cable that came with your camera to both your camera and to the computer. The shape and size of the cable's plugs are different for the camera end than for the computer end. You must plug in the ends that fit the connectors on the camera and computer.

3. Turn your computer and camera back on.

4. Use your computer's normal method for opening a program to open the image-editing program (in this case, Olympus CAMEDIA Master). You immediately see three windows (see Figure 6-2): at top left, a directory of the folders on your hard drive; beneath that, a window containing the My Camera icon; and beside both (if a directory containing images is currently selected), a window filled with miniature representations of those images. If there are no images in the selected directory, the main window will be empty.

Figure 6-2:   The CAMEDIA Master interface.

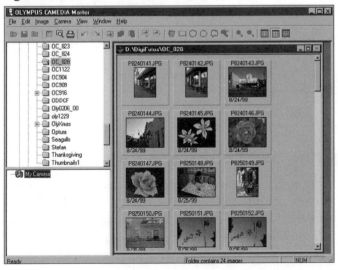

Installing and Getting Started in PhotoDeluxe

Here's how to install PhotoDeluxe, start it, and open a file containing the photos you took with your digital camera:

1. Place the PhotoDeluxe CD-ROM in your CD-ROM drive. If yours is a Windows computer, the installation program may start automatically. If you're using an older version of Windows or a Macintosh, open the CD-ROM in the usual way and double-click the Install icon. The install program gives you clear instructions for the rest of the installation process.

2. After the installation is complete, the installation program places an icon on your computer's main screen or desktop. Double-click that icon to start the program.

3. Click the Get & Fix Photo tab after the program opens. You will see a button bar at the top of the screen (refer to Figure 6-1). Click the Get Photo button.

4. Open the device that contains your photos. That could be direct from your digital camera, from a scanner attached to your system, from the Internet, or — most likely — from any of the disk drives attached to your computer.

5. If you have chosen a camera or disk drive, a typical file open dialog box appears. Select the file you want to load and click the OK button.

Correcting and Enhancing Your Photos

You no longer have to live with photos in which everyone has a demonic look with red eyes, things that you don't want other folks to see appear in the background, or you have a blemish on a subject's face. You can manipulate and correct your photos in your image-editing software. The remainder of this chapter explains how you can make changes to your photos by using PhotoDeluxe. Remember that you can use almost any other image-editing software to do these tasks as well.

Repairing photos and getting rid of artifacts and noise

Compression artifacts and other types of *noise* (grainy blotches of random or unfaithful color) are commonplace in digital photos. This is especially true if you have used a quality mode that permits storing more than the minimum number of pictures in your camera's memory. Figure 6-3 features a magnified part of an image that clearly shows what compression artifacts look like.

Figure 6-3:   The blotchy pixels in the sky are compression artifacts.

Actually, you can seldom annihilate compression artifacts, but here's how to minimize them:

1. In PhotoDeluxe, open the file you want to fix.

2. Click the Repair Photo button.

3. From the Repair Photo menu, choose Remove Noise.

4. A new set of tabs appears at the top of the screen: Graininess, Moiré, JPEG, and Done. The type of noise we want to remove is JPEG compression artifacts. In order to get to JPEG, you must choose each of the others in turn. If you click JPEG without clicking the others first, nothing happens.

5. From the JPEG tab, click the Clean Up JPEG button. A JPEG Clean Up dialog box appears. At the left side of the dialog box is a preview window. If necessary, click the + and - buttons below the image to set magnification at 1:1.

6. Move the cursor into the preview window. The cursor symbol turns to a hand, and you can drag until you can see the part of the image you want to fix.

7. Drag the Smoothness slider all the way to the left so you can see your artifacts in the preview window; then move the Smoothness slider to the right until you see the best compromise between sharp edges and no artifacts.

8. Click OK.

The other choices for cleanup are Graininess or Moiré. *Graininess* is a problem that arises when high-speed or overdeveloped film is scanned, resulting in visible clumps of the film's light-sensitive silver halide. *Moiré patterns* usually result when images are scanned from the pages of a publication.

Changing the overall color tint of your photos

Color balance problems result when your camera misinterprets the color of the prevalent light source. For instance, daylight and electronic flash (strobe) are quite blue in color, whereas most indoor lighting is quite yellow. If the camera saw one type of indoor lighting and you fired an external strobe, the *color balance* (overall tint) of your image would be yellow. You can correct this type of problem in your image-editing software.

The PhotoDeluxe program's Get & Fix Photo mode lets you fix color balance in three different ways. You can access all three ways by clicking the Adjust Quality button on the Get & Fix Photo taskbar (refer to Figure 6-1). One of these ways is called the IntelliFix Instant Fix command. This command automatically adjusts all the values in the image according to the program's estimate of what the brightness, contrast, color balance, and sharpness of the image should be. This process is always a good thing to try first. Even if you don't like the result, it may give you a good idea of how you'd like to adjust the image. You may also find that (much of the time) this is the only correction you need. If you don't like the result, immediately press ⌘/Ctrl+Z to undo it.

The other two methods for changing color balance are much better at letting you use your own selective judgement. These methods are Variations and Color Balance. Variations lets you pick the balance you like from a screenful of thumbnails. Color Balance lets you drag sliders to control the brightness of each primary color (Red, Green, and Blue) in the image.

Correcting bad exposure

Correcting for *overexposure* (a picture that's washed out) or *underexposure* (a picture that's too dark) is one of the things that PhotoDeluxe lets you do in several ways, ranging from dead simple to providing exacting control. None of this ever gets difficult, though. Here are the methods you can use:

- **IntelliFix:** A one-click, nonadjustable, simultaneous cure for bad color balance and over the range of tones from highlights-to-shadows.

- **Brightness and Contrast:** You move sliders while you preview the image and click OK when you approve of the changes.

To use either of these methods, follow these steps:

1. Open your photo in the Get & Fix Photo mode of PhotoDeluxe.

2. Click the Adjust Quality button. The Adjust Quality menu appears.

3. Choose Appearance from the Adjust Quality menu.

4. Either click the Instant Fix tab and then click the IntelliFix button, or move on to the Tune tab and click the Brightness and Contrast button. You can even work with IntelliFix first and then fine-tune the results with the Brightness/Contrast dialog box.

Eliminating Red Eye

Red eye is a phenomenon that occurs when you use the built-in flash on your digital camera without first using your camera's controls to choose the red-eye option. Of course, red eye also happens when you use cameras that don't have a red-eye option. Red eye happens because the pupils of the subject's eyes were enlarged to see better in dim light. Fortunately, red eye is a really easy thing to fix, as long as you have a starter-level image-editing program, such as PhotoDeluxe.

Here's how you use PhotoDeluxe to fix the problem:

1. In Get & Fix Photo mode, click the Repair Photo button.

2. Choose Remove Red Eye from the Repair Photo menu.

3. Click the Select tab and then drag a rectangular marquee around one of the eyes (see Figure 6-4).

Figure 6-4:   Placing a rectangular marquee around the red eye.

4. Click the Remove tab and then click the Remove Red Eye button as many times as it takes to completely remove the red eye.

5. Repeat Steps 3 and 4 for each of the other eyes in the picture.

6. When you're through, click the Done tab.

Don't overdo it with clicking the Remove button. If the eye starts to lose its sparkle, press ⌘/Ctrl+Z to back up a step.

Cropping for Better Composition

At times, you may need to make your photo a particular size, either so that it will fit into a favorite frame or because it needs to fit the layout for a greeting card, Web site layout, or printed publication. At the same time, you probably will need to make it a specific width and height, regardless of the height-to-width ratio of the original photo. For example, the height-to-width ratio of an 8-x-10-inch print is 1:1.25, while the height-to-width ratio of the typical 35mm or digital camera frame is 1:1.5.

An even better reason to trim the edges of your images is to quickly get rid of things you never cared to see. Trimming the edges of the image is called *cropping*. Cropping is also a way to improve the *composition* (arrangement of objects in relation to one another) of the picture by moving the center of interest closer to a point where the eye naturally wants to focus.

There are three reasons to trim and size a photo:

- To fit a specific size
- To fit specific proportions
- To include exactly the area you want to keep

Here's how to do any or all of the above:

1. In Get & Fix Photo mode, click the Rotate & Size button.

2. From the Rotate & Size menu, choose Trim & Size.

3. Choose the Trim tab. The Trim Size menu gives you a choice of cropping your image to a specific size. Even if you pick a size that requires a different number of *pixels* (picture elements) than the current image contains, PhotoDeluxe will intelligently recalculate the image to include the needed pixels. This recalculation is called *interpolation*. From the menu, pick the desired size.

Tip

If you don't care about height-to-width ratio or don't want to resize the image, no problem. Just choose the Any Size option in the Trim Size menu. You will then be able to change both the height and width of the marquee (the rectangle mentioned earlier).

4. A rectangle with four square handles appears in the image. You can change the area that the rectangle contains by dragging any of those handles. Notice that the height-to-width proportions remain the same (see Figure 6-5).

Figure 6-5: Trimming (cropping) the image to a specific size.

5. You can drag the rectangle to any position in the image.

6. After you're satisfied with the size of the rectangle and its position over the image, click the OK check mark in the Trim toolbar.

7. The image will be trimmed and interpolated to the size you choose in the menu.

Getting Rid of the Unsightly

The preceding is just one method of getting rid of stuff you didn't want in the picture: Trim it off. Now, what if you have things *inside* the cropped area (such as lawn trash or skin blemishes) that you want to "cover over"? You do just what 90 percent of the pro digital retouchers do: Use the Clone tool. A *Clone tool* is a brush that picks up the pixel pattern from one part of the image and then lets you brush that pixel pattern over another part of the image. So if you want to get rid of litter on the lawn, just choose a clean patch of grass as the pickup point and then paint the grass over the garbage.

Here's how to do it:

1. Open your photo in Get & Fix Photo mode; then click the Repair Photo button.

2. From the Repair Photo menu, choose either Retouch Face or Restore Old Photo. Both options operate in exactly the same way.

3. Click the Zoom tab and then click the Zoom button. Your cursor becomes a magnifier. Drag the cursor until you see a *marquee* (rectangular bounding box) that encloses the area you want to magnify. When you release the mouse button, the bounded portion of the image fills the window so that you can see the details you want to retouch.

4. Click the Repair tab and the Clone button. A small circle with a crosshair, called the *Sample Point,* appears in the image window.

5. Drag the Sample Point to an area that you want to copy over the blemish and click to anchor the Sample Point. The cursor immediately becomes a circle that indicates the current size of your brush.

6. Move the cursor over the area you want to retouch and paint (click and drag).

7. Repeat Steps 5 and 6 until you've repaired all the blemishes; then click the Done tab.

CHAPTER 7

PRINTING YOUR PHOTOS

IN THIS CHAPTER

- Printing from the computer
- Making prints that last
- Printing directly from the camera
- Sending images out for printing
- Making prints via the Internet
- Understanding the quality you can expect

I think that you'd agree that it doesn't do you much good to take pictures if you can't share them with others. Of course, the traditional way of doing that is by making prints. In the next chapter, you find out how to share them over the Internet. Meanwhile, you may find more choices than you ever imagined for sharing them the old-fashioned way (as prints).

Note: New printers, inks, and papers that make digital prints that last as long as conventionally made photographic color prints have recently been introduced. For more information on these developments, see "Making Prints That Last," later in this chapter.

Getting Prints That Look Like You Expected Them to Look

Setting up your camera and monitor so that you will see approximately the same qualities of your image on your screen as you see on paper can be simple (and virtually cost-free) unless you're a professional with exacting pre-press requirements. This process is called *monitor calibration*.

Many of the newest computers come with a small calibration program called Adobe Gamma. On the Macintosh and in Windows 98+, the settings you make in Adobe Gamma will calibrate the appearance of the monitor for all the applications you are running. Running Adobe Gamma is very easy. Just follow these steps:

1. In your system folder (or My Computer if you're using Windows), double-click the Adobe Gamma icon. This action brings up the opening screen.

2. On the opening screen, choose the Adobe Gamma Wizard button and click OK. Then, just follow the steps that the Wizard gives you for the rest of the application (see Figure 7-1).

Figure 7-1:   The Adobe Gamma Wizard.

If you don't have a Mac or are working in an older version of Windows that doesn't come with Adobe Gamma pre-installed your image-editing program may give you some means of calibrating your monitor that works only while you are in that specific application. If this is the case, you will have to check the documentation for that program. Adobe Gamma doesn't work on most laptop screens.

Printing from the Computer

Printing your digital photographs is, generally-speaking, easier and less costly if you first upload your images to a computer and then print them from your image-editing software. All image-editing software, regardless of cost — including whatever came bundled with your camera — is capable of sending output to a printer. There are also printers that let you place your camera's digital film card directly into the printer and then print the images without using a computer at all. However, these printers tend to cost a bit more, and many print in sizes that are too small to make them practical for printing such business documents as letters and spreadsheets.

Although many different printer manufacturers produce printers that are capable of making photo-quality prints, certain parts of the printmaking process will be consistent:

1. If you expect a print that's truly of photographic quality, make sure that you've purchased a paper that's clearly labeled "photo quality." The best papers are heavyweight papers and feel like the paper you see conventional photos printed on.

2. Follow the instructions in your printer's manual for installing the printer's driver software in your computer.

3. (Optional) If you are connected to the Web, visiting the printer manufacturer's Web site and seeing whether any updates have been made to the driver is a good idea. If updates have been made, follow the Web site's instructions for downloading and installing the updates.

4. Follow your operating system's procedure for choosing the printer you intend to use for printing photos. Note that some programs, such as Fax software, are treated as printers. Thus you may have to choose the right printer even if you think that you have only one printer attached to your computer.

5. Be sure that your image-editing software has been installed on your computer.

6. Open the file you want to print and make whatever changes you want to see in the final print.

7. In your image-editing application, choose File⇨Page Setup. A dialog box that allows you to choose among many different types of settings appears. I can't be more specific about how this dialog box will look, because each manufacturer writes its own dialog boxes. Be sure that you choose the proper paper type and size and make all the appropriate settings according to the recommendations of the printer's manufacturer. Usually, different settings are required for different papers and ink types. Read your printer's manual. After you've made the right settings in the Page Setup dialog box, click OK.

8. Choose File⇨Print. The Print dialog box appears. Check one more time to see that your paper size and orientation are correct. *Orientation* refers to whether you are printing in *Portrait* (the image is taller than it is wide) or *Landscape* (wider than tall) mode.

9. You may want to make settings for the start and end page (not usually the case when printing photos), color space, and certain others settings that may be peculiar to your printer. Once again, you'll need to read the manufacturer's recommendations.

10. Insert the paper in the printer and make sure that the printer is turned on.

11. Click the OK button in the Print dialog box. Your printer should begin printing.

Things you should know about printing a photograph

The method of printing a photograph from your image-editing program is nearly identical to that for printing a document from any of your computer's other programs. Of course, this presupposes that you have installed your printer and it's required software according to the printer's manual. The considerations that are unique to printing photographs that you want to take into account are the following:

- Size of the printed image on the printed page.

- Avoiding *banding* (horizontal white stripes across the image).

- Matching *inkflow* (the amount of ink sprayed over a given area) and paper type. This is important so that you don't get prints that are too light (not enough ink to compensate for the absorbency and whiteness of the paper) or that won't dry or where colors run together (likely to be a problem on very glossy papers and films that absorb very little ink).

- Image orientation. Do you want the image to be rotated to fit the proportions of the page?

- Setting the printer for the correct paper thickness. This avoids paper jams, which can ruin the printer (at worst) or the print (at best).

Assuming that the image you want to print has been opened in your image-editing software, here's how to make the settings that are likely to take care of the above considerations. These are the steps typical of an Epson printer, but other inkjet printers will be similar. You'll have to examine the manual for your specific printer in any case:

1. To set the size of the printed image on the printed page, divide the vertical resolution of the printer (in dots per inch) by three. If your printer is a contemporary Epson, the result will be 240 (720 vertical dpi divided by 3 = 240).

2. In your image-editing program, set the image size to an output resolution of 240 dpi. Generally, the image size will now be the image's current horizontal and vertical dimensions divided by 240.

3. To avoid banding, choose File⇨Page Setup. The Page Setup dialog box for your currently chosen printer appears.

4. Click on a button that says Properties (or Options) or something similar. Another dialog box opens. Look around for a setting called Microweave On and choose it. This setting insures that the printer will blend the dots created by each pass of the printhead so that ink is applied evenly from the top to the bottom of the page.

5. Matching inkflow to the paper surface is done by following paper manufacturer's suggestions as to the surface type to be chosen in the printer's Page Setup Properties dialog box. Look for a menu or icons that let you choose the media type (usually identifiable by labels, such as regular, coated, glossy, and glossy film).

6. Orientation of the image on the page is determined by choosing either Portrait (vertical) or Landscape (horizontal) in the Page Setup dialog box.

7. Setting the printer for the correct paper thickness is especially important if you're printing photos on double-weight photo papers (the most popular variety) or on such art paper surfaces as watercolor paper or canvas. In the Page Setup dialog box, look for a "manual feed" option and take advantage of it. You can now close the Page Setup dialog box.

8. Many printers will also have a physical setting for thicker papers. If you are using the thicker papers described in Step 7, check your printer's manual to see if this is the case for your printer. If so, use the setting for the thicker paper.

Choosing a printer

The most popular (and arguably the best) printers for photos are inkjet printers. All current models of color inkjets printers are capable of a decent job of printing photos. However, some inkjet printers are specifically targeted at the photographic market. The best photo-oriented inkjets are slower than the best office-oriented inkjets by 25 to 50 percent. However, unless you print a high volume of business documents, you'll likely find the best photo printers perfectly adequate for printing office documents.

Choosing inks

For the most part, you should choose the inks recommended by your printer's manufacturer. The nozzles that spray the ink on your paper are microscopically small. Any slight chemical imbalances or impurities can clog these nozzles and void the warranty on the printer.

Third-party inks can present another problem, too: They may be somewhat different in color. If that is the case, you'll have a difficult time getting predictable color balance in your prints.

Choosing paper

You have a much wider range of practical choices in papers than in inks. You can print photos with reasonable fidelity on ordinary paper and imbedded in the text of ordinary business documents. However, if you're printing photos for maximum quality, you'll want to use photo-weight papers that are coated to receive inkjet inks. Make sure that the papers are water-resistant (so that inks don't run if they become slightly damp from moisture in the atmosphere) and that inks are dry to the touch immediately after printing. Remember that photographs use much more ink than text does because (with photographs) the ink has to cover the entire surface of the paper.

Printing Directly from the Camera

Some printers can interface directly with your camera or enable you to print directly from a digital film card. Some will even do both. If you don't want to learn to use a computer, need to pass photos around instantly (like you would pass a Polaroid photo around), or want to be able to sell event photos as you shoot them, these printers might be the answer to your prayers.

If snapshot-sized photos are adequate, several companies (including Olympus) make small dye-sublimation printers that sell for between $250 and $600 each and print directly from a digital camera or from a digital film card. With this type of setup, the cost of printing is slightly higher than having prints made at your local fast-photo lab.

Epson makes a Lightfast printer (see "Making Prints That Last," later in this chapter), the 875, that takes PCMCIA, SmartMedia, and Compact Flash cards and can also be interfaced with your computer. This printer can make six-color Lightfast prints on 8.5-inch wide paper; it sells for just under $400 list. This printer would be a great device to use if you want to sell photos directly from an event.

Making Prints That Last

One of the great disadvantages of digital photographs has been that the digital prints made by most of the popular devices have had a very short life span when compared to photographic prints. Over the past couple of years, combinations of ink and paper have been appearing that, when used on some *service bureau* (companies that sell high-end output printing services to businesses and to the general public) quality printers (primarily those made by Iris), would last as long or longer than those made on photographic paper. Unfortunately, those prints and the printers that make them are far too expensive for most of us.

Of late, these more specialized inks are beginning to be made available for Epson inkjet printers. However, even when those inks are used on Epson inkjet printers, the printer has to be dedicated to that purpose. It is also a practical necessity to settle on one brand of ink and a fairly narrow range of papers.

Suddenly, all that is about to change. Epson has introduced two new printers that are made specifically for producing color prints that will last as long or longer than prints made on conventional Type-C color printing materials. These printers are the models 870 and 1270 (for tabloid-sized papers). At list prices of $299 and $499 respectively, these printers prove that archival printmaking is finally within the reach of those of us who'd simply like to be reassured that our family photos can be passed on to the next generation.

If you don't want to print your images on your own printer at home, you have another option. A printer that uses regular color photographic paper that must be developed after exposure is available at most professional photo labs and service bureaus. You can bring in a digital file on a Zip disk, Jaz cartridge, or CD-ROM, and the lab can make a regular photographic color print from this digital file. Although this process is often more expensive than home printing, large-size prints can be made if the file has the necessary detail.

Sending Images Out for Printing

At times, you may need prints that are too large or that need to be too lightfast (usually because you want to sell them as collectible art or historical documents) for your desktop printer to handle. If you have such requirements, you can take your images to a service bureau that specializes in making such prints. Until you've had experience with service bureaus and know exactly how to speak their language, using a service that is located conveniently enough for you to deal with in person is best. Always take along a print that you have made so that the service bureau has a visual idea of how you want your print to look. Check with local artists and see which service bureaus are their favorites. You're most likely to get the best results from service bureaus that specialize in custom printing for artists and photographers. Some service bureaus and pro photo labs have equipment that can print and develop large size images on regular color photo print paper. These kinds of prints look and feel just like regular color photographs.

Using Online Printing Services

One of the easiest and least-expensive ways to get prints (and they're actually made on conventional photographic paper, conventionally processed) is to order them from one of the online services that seem to be popping up at the rate of two per week. Many of these services are listed in Chapter 8. You see, for the most part, the same services that give you free space for sharing your photos on the Internet are also those that let you order prints.

These services generally make prints in sizes ranging from 4" x 6" (the typical fast-photo-lab snapshot size) at prices that range from $0.39 to about $3.50 for an 8" x 10" print. The usual procedure goes like this:

1. You upload your camera's JPEG files to an "album" on the online printing service's Web site.

2. You then fill in an online form that specifies what size the prints should be.

3. You are given the total cost of your order and shipping charges.

4. If you approve, you enter your credit card number.

5. Within three to five days, the photos are in your real-life (not electronic) mailbox.

Some 'brick and mortar' photo labs and camera stores offer similar services and prices for prints made from digital files.

Understanding the Quality Requirements for Prints

A direct correlation exists between the *resolution* (number of distinct picture elements or *pixels*) of an image and the quality you can expect to get from the device that prints it. A good rule to use with desktop inkjet printers is to divide the horizontal pixel-per-inch resolution of the printer you're printing on by three; then divide the horizontal resolution of your image by that number to get the horizontal size of the maximum quality print you can expect. This doesn't mean that you can't make a larger print that will still look acceptable. Digital photos don't have grain, but prints that are larger than the size determined by the formula will definitely lack definition. Also, you may find that some images will benefit (almost imperceptibly) by using somewhat higher resolution.

Finally, if you are outputting to dye sublimation or laser printers, most use an image resolution of 300 dpi.

CHAPTER 8

SHARING PHOTOS OVER THE INTERNET

IN THIS CHAPTER:

- Optimizing images for top Web performance
- E-mailing images
- Creating online albums
- Posting images to your own site
- Protecting your copyrights
- Making virtual reality panoramas

Getting your images onto the Web — either as illustrations for a Web site or as a way to place your photos in a location where you can easily share them with your friends and family — is no big deal. However, you do need to know a few things that can make your postings to the Web faster for you and for the people who will be looking at them. There are also a few ways of using your images on the Web that you may not be aware of.

Optimizing Images for Top Web Performance

The main trick for posting pictures to a Web site or for sending them with an e-mail message is to get the file size small enough so that even those folks with slow modems will be able to receive the entire image within a few seconds. The secrets are simple:

- Keep your image dimensions small
- Optimize images for minimum data size

Small dimensions

The smaller the physical dimensions of your photograph, all other things being equal, the smaller its file size. The smaller the file size, the faster the image can move across the Web and open in the viewer's browser. You should also remember that more than half of the world's computer users use 13- to 15-inch monitors that have a maximum dimension of 640 pixels x 480 pixels. By the time you fit the browser's borders and menus into place, the maximum usable screen size is more like 550 pixels x 300 pixels. Figure 8-1 shows a browser window on a VGA (640 pixels x 480 pixels) screen. You can see the maximum size of an image outlined inside. Usually, you'll want your images to be even smaller. A typical maximum size for a featured illustration or portfolio image is about 350 pixels high and 500 pixels wide. Photos used as thumbnails, catalog items, or margin illustrations will be a fraction of that size, with the exact size to be dictated by the design of your Web pages.

Optimizing JPEGs

Photographic images, also known as *bitmaps*, can be recorded in many different file formats. However, only two of these file formats will work on the Web and also show the full range of colors and shades that can be seen in most photos: JPEG and PNG. JPEG is the same format most digital cameras use for storing their images (though a few cameras will let you save to an uncompressed TIF). JPEG is also, by far, the most commonly used file format and is understood by Web browsers. For that reason, you should almost always use the JPEG format. File formats are discussed in Chapter 5.

The trick is that JPEG lets you employ many different levels of file size reduction. The smaller the file, the greater the increase in *compression artifacts* (blotchy areas of color). However, because the Web is a low-resolution medium (typically 72 to 96 dots per inch), you can get away with quite a bit of data loss before the loss of quality becomes noticeable. Of course, just how much quality loss is acceptable is a matter of individual perception.

Figure 8-1: The maximum size of a Web photo after making room for browser menus and borders is 612 pixels x 288 pixels.

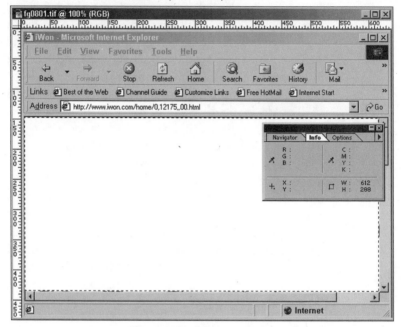

Ordinarily, the only way you can get it right is to save your file as JPEG under several different names (add a number to each save) while using a lower level quality setting each time. Then use your image editor to open all the files at the same time so that you can compare them side-by-side. Delete all the files that are of less-than-acceptable quality. Delete all but the smallest of the remaining files.

To save a file as JPEG from any image editor, follow these steps:

1. From the program's main menu, choose File⇨Save As. A file saving dialog box appears.

2. Enter a filename that you'd like to save the file as.

3. At the bottom of the dialog box is a pull-down menu that enables you to choose from any of several different file formats (including the TIFF, PNG, and GIF formats also mentioned in this chapter). Choose JPEG and click OK. A JPEG Options dialog box (it may have another, similar name) opens.

4. Use the Settings dialog box to determine the quality (compression) level you want to use. Programs vary in how much control you are given, but generally you can move a slider from minimum to maximum quality.

5. Indicate whether you want to use progressive scanning (see the info given in the paragraph beside the next Tip icon) when the image is displayed in a browser.

6. Click OK to save the file.

If you plan to make lots of Web images, you'll find that you can save a considerable amount of time by using a program made for the purpose of optimizing JPEGs. The two most popular of these programs are Adobe Image Ready (now part of Photoshop 5.5+) and Macromedia Fireworks. Both programs let you see as many as four different levels of optimization before you decide which to save as your final Web-destined file. Pricing for software for optimizing JPEGs ranges from about $30 for most shareware programs to just under $200 for Macromedia Fireworks. The more expensive programs are from mainstream manufacturers and enable you to see as many as four different optimizations of the same file *before* you save. They are also intended as all-purpose programs for preparing Web graphics; GIF optimization, animated GIF authoring, image-slicing, buttons and rollover events, and making image maps are all capabilities that are included.

What's this about PNG?

If you want to place very-high-quality images on the Web to be reviewed for professional purposes or if you need to create *masked* (irregularly-shaped) images without compromising image quality, you'll have to resort to the PNG (Portable Network Graphics) format. PNG is a new format that can be recognized only by the latest generation (or two) of browsers without first having installed special plug-in software. Only the most recent generation of image-editing programs is likely to be capable of saving to PNG format.

E-Mailing Images

Starting with Version 4 of Netscape Navigator and Internet Explorer, you can attach a JPEG image to any e-mail message, and the picture will be visible when the reader scrolls to the bottom of the e-mail message. In either browser, you can also use your computer's Paste command to place an image right into the text.

Attaching an image to an e-mail message is really easy. Here's how:

1. In your e-mail program, enter the address of the recipient and the subject of the e-mail in their appropriate fields.

2. Enter the text of your message in the area reserved for that purpose. This step is optional and can take place after you've attached the image.

3. Locate the icon or menu command that lets you make attachments. It's usually given an obvious label, such as Attach (Internet Explorer). A file-opening-type dialog box of the type that's standard for your computer's operating system will appear.

4. Locate the directory in which the image file you wish to attach has been stored and double-click its folder icon to open it.

5. Locate the file you wish to attach and double-click its filename or icon. The dialog boxes will close, and you will see a message at the top of your e-mail message to show that the file has been attached.

6. Choose the Send command or click the send button in your e-mail program.

Some older browsers may not display the images. Even in that case, you can open the image by double-clicking its filename where it appears in your e-mail program as an attachment.

Creating Online Albums

Finally, you can place photo albums on the Web so that they can be shared with others, even if you don't have a Web site of your own. You just tell your friends and family the Web address to visit to see the photos. Most firms charge no fee for doing this.

There are many photo-dot-com companies. They tend to come in three varieties:

- **Photo communities:** They permit you to post photos online and hope that you and your friends will order prints or photo gifts from the pictures.

- **Online photo labs:** These are firms that you e-mail your digital pictures to expressly for making prints or photo gifts from the images.

- **Photo retailers who are selling hardware on the Web:** They may also have a digital photo print service too.

All of these also offer "photo know-how" content pages on how to be a better photographer and the like.

The following is a list of Web sites that allow you to publish your photo albums at no charge. Instructions for doing so will be clearly posted on each of these sites:

- **ClubPhoto:** www.clubphoto.com

- **eMemories:** www.ememories.com

- **Kablink:** www.kablink.com

- **Kodak PhotoNet online:** www.kodak.com/US/en/photoNet/aol

- **Ofoto:** www.ofoto.com (The first 50 prints are free.)

- **PhotoIsland:** www.photoisland.com

- **PhotoLoft.com:** www.photoloft.com

- **PhotoPoint.com:** www.photopoint.com (Also has many online articles about digital photography as well as an online photo store.)

- **PrintRoom.com:** www.printroom.com

- **Zing:** www.zing.com

Posting Images to Your Own Site

One of the nicest ways to share photos is to place them on a Web site; then simply send an e-mail message to everyone that you want to have see the images and include a link to the site where the pictures reside. Creating a page of thumbnail (postage-stamp-size) images and then establishing a postage-stamp-size link from each small image to a page that contains only one (or very few) larger images is best. That way, your correspondents can see the detail in the images that most interest them.

Any easy-to-use visual Web site editor will make creating these albums easy. A few of the many such editors in widespread use are Adobe PageMill and GoLive, Claris HomePage, Macromedia Dreamweaver, and Microsoft Frontpage.

There's an even easier way to post images to your own site, however: Use an image-management program that automatically creates online albums (see Chapter 9). You follow the program's standard (and very easy) procedure for creating a thumbnail catalog; then you simply make a menu choice to save that catalog to HTML pages.

Protecting Your Copyrights

Because you may want to post your photos to Web sites, have them published, or otherwise make them visible to the general public, you may be concerned about preventing them from being used or abused by others without your permission.

If you distribute prints, always make sure that they are marked on the back with your copyright information. This copyright information should include the copyright symbol (circle enclosing a *c*), the date the image was made public, followed by the name of the photographer. Do the same on any Web page that displays your photos.

An even more secure way to protect digital photos is available: digital watermarking. Digimarc Corporation is one of several companies that make software that enables you to embed an invisible copyright in your image — a copyright that cannot be seen but can be detected even if the image has been cropped or manipulated. The software is integrated into several image-editing programs including Adobe Photoshop, iGrafx PicturePublisher, and JASC PaintShop Pro. You do need to concern yourself with some limitations:

- Image compression shouldn't be too lossy. If you're saving to JPEG, it's best not to use compression levels below 50 percent.

- Image size should be at least 100 pixels square.

- *Durability settings* (which determine how much image manipulation the watermark can take before becoming unreadable and which the software lets you choose when you embed the watermark) should be set at a fairly high level when using JPEG.

Making Virtual Reality Panoramas

Many digital cameras come with software that lets you stitch together multiple images into a panorama that can be saved to a file format called QuickTime VR. This QuickTime VR file can then be placed into a Web page in the same way as any other photo. People whose browsers are equipped with QuickTime VR plug-ins can then view the panorama by using their mouse to scroll a 360-degree view and to zoom in and out on the image. Figure 8-2 shows an image that has been stitched together from several images.

Figure 8-2: An image stitched together from several images.

Putting panoramas together is easiest when you use programs intended for that purpose. Except for PowerStitch, which is intended for very high-resolution professional panoramas, these programs are all quite affordable and very easy to use. Although their interfaces differ significantly, the basic procedure goes something like this:

1. Name the files you will use with the name of the scene followed by a sequential number. Most programs can use this information to arrange the frames in the panorama in the proper left-to-right sequence automatically.

2. Open the panorama program and then open the images that compose the panorama. You may have to use some method of rearranging the files in proper sequence.

3. Drag the images into position so that they overlap at approximately the right points.

4. Tell the panorama program to stitch the panorama together.

5. View the panorama and check for problems.

6. Export the panorama to the file format(s) you want to use.

Stitching software can be purchased (separately from the camera) from the following firms:

- **Apple Computer:** QuickTime VR Authoring Studio $395.00

- **Enroute Imaging:** QuickStitch $49.95 or PowerStitch $399.95

- **MGI Software:** PhotoVista $59.95 or Reality Studio $129.95

When photographing images to be stitched into a panorama, you should use a tripod and make sure that it is level. Then rotate the camera, taking overlapping photos of the circular view that you want. You can't make accurate overlapping images by handholding the camera. Setting the exposure manually so that it doesn't change as the camera revolves is also a good idea. Be sure to have a 20- to 50-percent overlap in images from one frame to the next. Finally, orienting the camera vertically and shooting more pictures is best. Vertical orientation gives you a wider angle of view from top to bottom.

Animating Photographs

At first, using photographs for Web animations may not seem practical. The most popular file format for Web animation is the animated GIF, which limits you to 256 colors. However, if the images are small and/or if the image-editing program that is used to optimize the GIF is good at intermingling the color dots, you can make photos look quite acceptable. Simple animations, such as raising an eyebrow or winking, are easily accomplished with one or two photographs.

Most programs that make animated GIFs can also be used to make images appear to move into view from off-screen and into place in rows and columns or stacked atop one another. You can use these techniques for building a more dynamic interface or thumbnail page for a photographic portfolio. Both Image Ready and Fireworks have GIF animation capabilities built into them.

An even more exciting possibility is placing true-color, full-sized photographs into Macromedia Flash and then using that program's animation capabilities. One benefit is that you can use full-color photos instead of GIFs. Of course, the larger size of Macromedia Flash images and the increased data needed for interpreting more colors can slow Web performance to a crawl, but this isn't a problem if your target audience uses wide-band Internet connections (such as DSL, cable, ISDN, or T-1). You can also use Flash to create content for offline use, such as games and CD-ROMs.

CHAPTER 9
ORGANIZING YOUR DIGITAL PHOTOS

IN THIS CHAPTER

- Introducing image-management software
- Naming files
- Organizing file folders
- Printing proofs
- Making thumbnails

One of the most persistent annoyances inherent in digital photography (and digitized photographs) is the difficulty of finding exactly the image you need at the moment you need it. This becomes especially true after you've extensively taken advantage of the fact that digital pictures are free (so why not take lots of them?). The most helpful thing you can do is to create the digital equivalent of a photographer's contact sheets. *Contact sheets* display small versions (*thumbnails*) of all the images on a roll (or digital camera memory card) and their frame numbers on a single page (or computer screen). In other words, you need to establish a visual catalog of your images so that you can tell which of the 447 photographs of yellow roses is the one with the bee pollinating the pistils.

Much more can be done to make finding the right photo easier. How much more you want to do depends on how much time and additional software you want to invest in such an effort. The outcome of that decision will probably depend on how much your time is worth and how many photos you plan to make.

Working with What You've Got

If you don't own image-management software and don't find that you can justify its purchase, know that you can still follow some image-management procedures that will make life lots easier for you. Here's a list of things you should do regardless of what software you have:

■ Give your files names that help you remember their contents and when they were shot. Remember that you have the opportunity to name your files when you save them to your computer's hard drive.

■ Use filenames that can be read on all types of computers (see "Naming Files," later in this chapter).

■ Organize your files into directories by date, location, or subject. (You can even organize them in all three ways if you like.)

■ Print contact sheets so that you can find your files visually.

Naming Files

Your digital camera will probably name your files with a letter followed by eight sequential numbers, a period, and an additional three letters that indicate the graphics file format. If you're lucky, the sequential number is related to the date the picture was taken, but that's only true of some cameras under some circumstances. The point is that numbers, such as P013100.JPG, aren't easily remembered as belonging to any particular subject. What if you have to find a photo in a hurry and all you have to go on is several hundred such numbers? Your operating system may give you a small visual preview, but it's still too small to be much help. The bottom line is this: The first thing you should do after downloading pictures from your camera to your computer is to open the files so that you can see the pictures and then rename the file according to its contents.

Giving your individual shots a five-letter name that identifies the subject as closely as possible is a good idea. Why five letters? So that you will have three letters left over for numbering up to 999 different photos of the same subject — thus making it possible to differentiate between frames of the same subject. For instance, if a picture is of a flower, name it *flowr001* or *rose001*.

Why be so brief? Most modern operating systems let you use filenames that are at least 35 characters long, and you can include all sorts of symbols and even spaces in those filenames. Isn't that much more descriptive? The problem lies in two important areas: The Internet and CD-ROMs. You can be certain that any browser, Web server, or computer will recognize an eight-letter+three-letter-extension (separated by a period — or "dot") filename. The same is true for CD-ROMs. Any computer can read eight-letter filenames with three-letter extensions — alphanumeric characters only — no symbols or spaces allowed. (You can use an underline character to separate names.)

Of course, you can use long filenames until you need to post an image on a Web page or save it to a cross-platform CD. It's just that if you do use long filenames, you'll spend hours renaming dozens or hundreds of files when you get ready to put your files on a Web site or CD-ROM that must be readable by any type of computer.

Organizing file folders

Because short filenames are best, having other ways to locate files quickly can help. One way to organize images is to place them in file folders (subdirectories) by subject, purpose, date, or client (for example, *flowers* or *garden* or *041400* or *Texaco*). If you have enough storage space (or a removable media drive, such as a CD-ROM recorder), you may even want to copy some files into several different folders, thus making finding files by several different criteria much easier.

Printing proofs

Images on computers haven't replaced photos on paper any more than text on computers has replaced the printed word on paper. Believe me, if you've organized your images as I've suggested so far, you can find them a lot faster if you've also printed out proofs on paper. Such proofs should consist of rows and columns of thumbnails, typically about sixteen to a page, with the name of each file appearing below the thumbnail.

Most image-editing software provides a means for you to make such proofs. Ironically, Photoshop 5.5, the professional's choice, is one of the least capable in this regard. Adobe PhotoDeluxe (Mac and Windows) Corel PHOTO-PAINT 9, JASC Paint Shop Pro, Ulead PhotoExpress, MGI PhotoSuite, Microsoft Picture It!, and MicroFrontier's Color It! (Mac only) are just a few that will give you an automated means of doing the job.

Making Thumbnails

Even if your image-editing program doesn't automate the process of making proof sheets, chances are excellent that the software that came with your digital camera makes proof sheets automatically. Olympus's Camedia, which is included with the company's entire line of digital cameras, uses an interface similar to that of the Windows Explorer or Microsoft's Internet Explorer to guide you to the desired folder (see Figure 9-1). The following part of this chapter presents information on various software programs that enable you to make thumbnails.

Figure 9-1: Camedia automatically makes thumbnails of all the images in any folder you open.

Using what comes with your camera

Basically, two types of software come with digital cameras; each type functionally overlaps the other to at least some degree. The difference between them is one of emphasis and priorities:

■ **Image managers:** These programs start out by showing you the contents of a film card or directory folder as thumbnails. They are typified by Olympus's Camedia — but some other manufacturers have software with similar functionality.

■ **Image editors:** These programs are generally very basic image editors that also come with some means of creating a thumbnail catalog. The most popular of these is Adobe PhotoDeluxe.

Probably the best time to give your photos memorable and identifiable names is as soon as you've made a thumbnail catalog. You can then select the image visually, press a button or click an icon, and type in a new name for the image at the same time that you can see and compare it with other similar images that were shot at the same time and location.

Using ThumbsPlus

ThumbsPlus is a shareware program for Windows that operates very much like Olympus Camedia. The difference is that anyone can download and use ThumbsPlus, and the registration fee is a very moderate $29.95. You don't have to tell ThumbsPlus to make thumbnails; you just use the navigation window to find a folder that contains images. As soon as you select the folder, the images appear in the right-hand window (as shown in Figure 9-2). You can access the Cerious Software (the company that makes ThumbsPlus) Web site at www.cerious.com.

Figure 9-2:   The ThumbsPlus window.

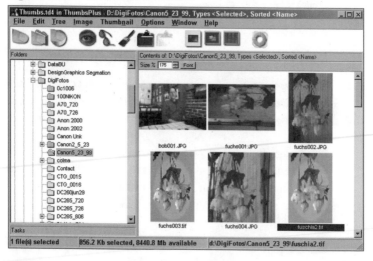

Several of these programs, including EasyPhoto and Thumbs-Plus, enable you to number a group of sequential files automatically. You select the files for which you want to have the same letters in common; then you choose whatever that particular program calls its auto-rename command. A dialog box that enables you to enter the characters that all the files will have in common appears. You are then asked to enter the beginning number in the sequence. (You could enter 03- for

March, for example.) The program then automatically adds sequential numbers, so your files would be numbered bob03-01, bob03-02, and the like.

Using Extensis Portfolio

Extensis Portfolio, Canto Cumulus, and other *professional asset-management* (image management plus management of all sorts of multimedia files) *software* work on both Macs and Windows computers and are capable of maintaining a much wider range of data associated with each image (or other asset). Both Extensis Portfolio and Canto Cumulus are also available in versions that let you share images across networks.

You can discover much more about Extensis Portfolio (and can download a fully functional 30-day trial version) by logging on to the Extensis Web site at www.extensis.com. To use Portfolio 5.0 for making thumbnails, follow these steps:

1. Open the Portfolio program. A Welcome to Portfolio dialog box appears.

2. Select the Create a New Portfolio Catalog radio button and click OK. A New Catalog dialog box appears.

3. The New Catalog dialog box is a conventional file-opening dialog box. Just find the folder you want to catalog and double-click the folder to open it.

4. While the New Catalog dialog box is still open, enter the filename you'd like to give this catalog. If you don't enter an extension, Portfolio adds the .fdb extension for you.

5. Click OK. The catalog window opens in Portfolio.

6. Choose Catalog⇨Add Items (or press ⌘/Ctrl+E). An Add Items dialog box appears — yet another standard file-loading dialog box. This Add Items dialog box presents several options; but for the most part, you'll want to add all the assets in a particular folder.

7. Navigate to the folder you want to catalog and double-click its name to open it.

8. Finally, click the Current Folder button. The Cataloging Options dialog box appears.

9. The Cataloging Options dialog box is your first real clue as to the potential power of Portfolio. To make thumbnails of all the files in the folder that you want to catalog, click OK. A Cataloging Status dialog box appears and shows you the progress being made in creating each thumbnail. Just watch and wait until the process completes itself. When it does, you'll have results like those you see in Figure 9-3.

Figure 9-3:   A thumbnail catalog created in Portfolio.

CLIFFSNOTES REVIEW

Use this CliffsNotes Review to practice what you've learned in this book and to build your confidence in doing the job right the first time. After you work through the review questions, the problem-solving exercises, and the fun and useful practice projects, you're well on your way to achieving your goal of taking and sharing digital photographs.

Q&A

1. One of the outstanding characteristics of digital photography is:

  a. Ultrahigh image definition

  b. No film cost

  c. Capability to synchronize with external flash units

2. How is the amount of detail your camera can capture commonly stated by the camera's maker? _____ _____

3. Name two limitations of the LCD preview monitor.

  _____ _____

4. What are the four most common operating modes for setting your built-in light meter? _____ _____

5. Which of the following is not an industry-standard type of removable-memory digital film?

  a. CompactFlash

  b. SmartMedia

  c. PCMCIA card (also known as a PC card)

  d. Sony Memory Stick

6. Which of the following is not a device for downloading pictures to your computer?

a. Card reader

b. USB or serial cable

c. Parallel cable

7. As a general rule, where should you place the center-of-interest within the viewfinder frame for the actual exposure?

a. In the center

b. One-third the distance between one side of the frame and the other

c. Anywhere, as long as you can see the whole thing

8. Assuming that your camera lets you use the LCD preview monitor as a viewfinder, when is it not best to do that?

a. When you are only a few feet from your subject

b. When you're shooting action in very bright light

c. When you want to see exactly what the film sees

Answers: (1) b. (2) By the number of megapixels. (3) It is difficult to see in bright light and lacks enough resolution for accurate focus. (4) Auto, center-weighted, spot, and matrix. (5) d. (6) c. (7) c. (8) b.

Scenarios

1. You are photographing a family member late in the afternoon. The most important thing to remember is to _____.

2. You are about to embark on your first digital camera shoot. To prepare for it, you should _____.

3. You are shooting outdoors when the sun is at a low angle. To avoid lens flare, you should _____.

4. You are photographing a friend in bright sunlight, so the shadows are very dark in comparison to the highlights. To minimize the difference so that you can see detail in both areas, you should _____.

Answers: (1) Keep the sun behind you. (2) Read your camera's manual, install fully charged batteries, and make sure that you've inserted the film card. (3) Keep the sun from shining directly onto the surface of the lens. A sunshade can be very helpful. (4) Set your camera's flash mode for automatic fill flash or use a reflector to bounce light back into the shadows.

Visual Test

The photo in Figure 1 demonstrates the most common mistakes that beginning photographers make when shooting portraits in dim light. Can you state three things the photographer could have done to improve the shot?

Figure 1: On-camera flash.

Answers: Soften the on-camera flash by covering it with crumpled white tissue or tracing paper. Use the camera's red-eye reduction flash mode, which is available on most, but not all, digital cameras. If possible, given the limitations of your camera, use an external flash unit and raise the light source above and to one side of the subject. Place the model in front of a plainer or simpler background, such as a solid color wall.

Consider This

■ Did you know that you can use your LCD preview monitor in bright sunlight if you purchase an auxiliary hood that blocks out the sunlight and reflections? You can find out about such inexpensive and useful accessories by subscribing to the Digicam Digest, an e-mail list server. Visit www.leben.com.

■ Did you know that there are several Web sites that regularly review the latest developments in "affordable" digital cameras? Three of these are Steve's Digicams (www.shortcourses.com), Phil Askey's Digital Photography Review (photo.askey.net), and the author's Web site (www.kenmilburn.com).

Practice Project

1. Organize the pictures in one of your file folders. Start by giving the files eight-letter names. Use a thumbnail program (such as ThumbsPlus, Portfolio, or the program that came with your camera) to make a visual catalog of the images in that folder.

2. Take a two-hour practice picture jaunt. Go someplace local that you consider to be picturesque (or, at least, worth photographing) that's also lit by outdoor light. After you've finished photographing and have uploaded your pictures to your computer, study each photograph. For each picture, make a list of what you could have done to make the picture better. Use this book as a guide. Your chances of getting a good picture will improve several hundred percent.

CLIFFSNOTES RESOURCE CENTER

The learning doesn't need to stop here (and probably shouldn't). Quantum strides are being made in the technology that drives photography, so you'll find that it pays to keep up. CliffsNotes Resource Center shows you the best of the best — links to the best information in print and online about digital photography. And don't think that this is all we've prepared for you; we've put all kinds of pertinent information at www.cliffsnotes.com. Look for all the terrific resources at your favorite bookstore or local library and on the Internet. When you're online, make your first stop www.cliffsnotes.com where you'll find more incredibly useful information about digital photography and the printing of digital photographs.

Books

This CliffsNotes book is one of many great books about digital photography published by IDG Books Worldwide, Inc. So if you want some great next-step books, check out these other publications:

Digital Photography For Dummies, 3rd Edition, by Julie Adair King, is an excellent beginner's guide to digital photography by a seasoned professional photographer. A good guide to lighting and retouching, if you're planning on getting a little more serious. IDG Books Worldwide, Inc. $24.99.

Digital Photography Bible, by Ken Milburn, is the most comprehensive book yet on digital photography, including introductory coverage of professional equipment for digital photography. Extensive coverage of more-specialized software and equipment for the serious hobbyist or business professional. IDG Books Worldwide, Inc. $39.99.

Master Photoshop 5.5 VISUALLY, by Ken Milburn, is a very helpful quick reference to solving problems in photography by using Adobe Photoshop 5.5 — including Image Ready 2.0 for Web imaging. All the steps are visually illustrated in a very-easy-to-follow manner. IDG Books Worldwide, Inc. $39.99.

Real World Digital Photography, by Deke McClelland and Katrin Eismann, is an in-depth guide to digital photography for those who take it seriously or need to put it to use in business. Peachpit Press, $44.99.

It's easy to find books published by IDG Books Worldwide, Inc., and Peachpit Press. You'll find them in your favorite bookstores (on the Internet and at a store near you). We also have three Web sites that you can use to read about all the books we publish:

- www.cliffsnotes.com
- www.dummies.com
- www.idgbooks.com

Internet

Check out these Web sites for more information about digital photography and related equipment and software. All of these sites also have links to online camera stores, image sharing sites, and online print-making sites:

Dennis Curtin's Short Courses, www.shortcourses.com/index.htm, features courses on digital photography and the use of digital cameras. This site is a vast wealth of up-to-date information on digital photography, including free quick-reference pocket guides for nearly every digital camera.

Digital Eyes, www.image-acquire.com, specializes in news and reviews. It features short news blurbs that can be read quickly on many late-breaking developments.

Digital Photo Corner, www.dpcorner.com, is run by Arthur Bleich, one of the contributing editors to *Digital Camera Magazine*. Like all the sites mentioned previously, this site contains reviews of current digital cameras. This site distinguishes itself in the discovery of useful accessories. It also features a comparison of Epson printers.

Imaging Resource, www.imaging-resource.com, features very up-to-date camera reviews. You can compare output from reviewed cameras side-by-side. The site is also a wealth of other information on digital photography — especially when it comes to helpful articles on esoteric applications of digital photography.

Ken Milburn's Site, www.kenmilburn.com/digiphoto, is the author's Web site for posting the latest developments in digital photography, more helpful hints, links to other digital photography sites, and reviews of recently introduced equipment.

Steve's Digicams, www.steves-digicams.com, is another Web site that's a favorite among digital photographers who want up-to-date information from an experienced pro. Includes sections on accessories, digital camcorders (video cameras), and camera reviews from users.

Next time you're on the Internet, don't forget to drop by www.cliffsnotes.com. We created an online Resource Center that you can use today, tomorrow, and beyond.

Magazines on Digital Photography

This is a list of the periodicals that specialize in digital photography. These magazines are quite varied in their target audiences. You can find subject matter for any level of user from beginner to seasoned professional photographer.

Digital Camera Magazine at dcm.photopoint.com. This is a print magazine that also has a Web edition. It is especially valuable for its ability to show the printed results of digital photos. It features reviews of cameras, accessories, software, and books and also has instructional feature articles on various aspects of digital photography. Aeon Publishing Group, 88 Sunnyside Blvd., Suite 203, Plainview, NY 11803.

Digital Imaging at www.digitalimagingmag.com. This slim magazine bills itself as being for the "imaging professional" and features in-depth articles and reviews on all the technologies relating to digital photography. This is a good place to look into the limits you can push if you've got the time and money. Cygnus Publishing, 1233 Janesville Ave., P.O. Box 803, Fort Atkinson, WI .53538.

PC Photo at www.pcphotomag.com is aimed squarely at the digital photo hobbyist. It is chock full of worthwhile tips. Wemer Publishing Corp. 12121 Wilshire Blvd., Ste. 1200, Los Angeles, CA 90025.

PEI (Photo Electronic Imaging) Magazine at www.peimag.com is another publication aimed at pros and advanced hobbyists. Don't let that stop you. This magazine has some of the most knowledgeable reviews and hottest tips and tricks you'll find, written by some of the gurus of the industry. PEI Magazine, 229 Peachtree St. NE, Suite 2200, International Tower, Atlanta, GA 30303.

Photo District News (PDN) at www.pdn-pix.com presents a large format, luxuriously printed magazine aimed at the professional photography community. This magazine always has articles on various aspects of digital photography, often covering topics in depth that are of interest to any digital photographer, and features stunning examples of the best in digital photography. A sister quarterly publication, *PIX*, is devoted entirely to professional digital photography. PDN - Photo District News, 1515 Broadway, New York, NY, 10036; phone 212-536-5222.

Send Us Your Favorite Tips

In your quest for learning, have you ever experienced that sublime moment when you figure out a trick that saves time or trouble? Perhaps you realized you were taking ten steps to accomplish something that could have taken two. Or you found a little-known workaround that gets great results. If you've discovered a useful tip that helped you take and print digital photos more effectively and you'd like to share it, the CliffsNotes staff would love to hear from you. Go to our Web site at www.cliffsnotes.com and click the Talk to Us button. If we select your tip, we may publish it as part of CliffsNotes Daily, our exciting, free e-mail newsletter. To find out more or to subscribe to a newsletter, go to on the Web.

INDEX

NOTES

NOTES

NOTES

CliffsNotes™

Your shortcut to
success™
for over 40 years

Computers and Software
Confused by computers? Struggling with software? Let *CliffsNotes* get you up to speed on the fundamentals — quickly and easily. Titles include:

Balancing Your Checkbook with Quicken®
Buying Your First PC
Creating a Dynamite PowerPoint® 2000 Presentation
Making Windows® 98 Work for You
Setting up a Windows® 98 Home Network
Upgrading and Repairing Your PC
Using Your First PC
Using Your First iMac™
Writing Your First Computer Program

The Internet
Intrigued by the Internet? Puzzled about life online? Let *CliffsNotes* show you how to get started with e-mail, Web surfing, and more. Titles include:

Buying and Selling on eBay®
Creating Web Pages with HTML
Creating Your First Web Page
Exploring the Internet with Yahoo!®
Finding a Job on the Web
Getting on the Internet
Going Online with AOL®
Shopping Online Safely